Cyberboss

ι

Craig Gent is a writer, editor and researcher, as well as a Director at Novara Media. He was previously a Postdoctoral Fellow at the University of Warwick, and his work has been published in *Jacobin*, *Vice* and the *Independent*.

Cyberboss

*The Rise of Algorithmic
Management and the New Struggle
for Control at Work*

Craig Gent

VERSO

London • New York

First published by Verso 2024
© Craig Gent 2024

1 3 5 7 9 10 8 6 4 2

Verso
UK: 6 Meard Street, London W1F 0EG
US: 388 Atlantic Avenue, Brooklyn, NY 11217
versobooks.com

Verso is the imprint of New Left Books

ISBN-13: 978-1-83976-855-2
ISBN-13: 978-1-83976-857-6 (US EBK)
ISBN-13: 978-1-83976-856-9 (UK EBK)

British Library Cataloguing in Publication Data
A catalogue record for this book is available from the British Library

Library of Congress Cataloging-in-Publication Data

Names: Gent, Craig, author.
Title: Cyberboss : the rise of algorithmic management and the new struggle
    for control at work / Craig Gent.
Description: London ; New York, NY : Verso, 2024. | Includes
    bibliographical references.
Identifiers: LCCN 2024009814 (print) | LCCN 2024009815 (ebook) | ISBN
    9781839768552 (paperback) | ISBN 9781839768576 (ebook)
Subjects: LCSH: Management--Data processing. | Work environment.
Classification: LCC HD30.2 .G467 2024 (print) | LCC HD30.2 (ebook) | DDC
    658/.05--dc23/eng/20240316
LC record available at https://lccn.loc.gov/2024009814
LC ebook record available at https://lccn.loc.gov/2024009815

Typeset in Sabon by Biblichor Ltd, Scotland
Printed and bound by CPI Group (UK) Ltd, Croydon CR0 4YY

To all 'slaves to the algorithm'.

And in memory of Mark Fisher – a father,
husband, friend and comrade who is missed.

Contents

1. The Stakes   1
2. Algorithmic Work   14
3. Management   62
4. Technological Politics   109
5. Algorithmic Management   138
6. Guile against Adversity   176
7. Epilogue   209

   Acknowledgements   212
   Notes   214
   Index   241

1

The Stakes

Emancipatory politics must always destroy the appearance of a 'natural order', must reveal what is presented as necessary and inevitable to be a mere contingency, just as it must make what was previously deemed to be impossible seem attainable.
– Mark Fisher, *Capitalist Realism*

There is a growing sense that the future of work might not unfold in our favour. People are expected to work longer, for less, with less security and fewer protections. Rather than making work easier or more rewarding, we expect the development and application of new technologies, particularly in the areas of automation, computation and artificial intelligence, to disempower us. Concerns around the degradation of work are not new, but our everyday experience of moving through the world over the last ten or fifteen years tells us that many of the jobs that are now being created are less secure, more stringently managed and paid worse, relative to the cost of living, than ever before. It is commonly understood that this world of work has some relation to the proliferation of computational or algorithmic technologies, which are being applied to work in novel ways. Indeed, digital technologies appear to be changing the world of work at a fundamental level. Left unchecked, they may well lead to forms of work that are increasingly stressful, injurious and dehumanising.

My interest in the workplace as a site of politics began around eighteen years ago, when, as a teenager, I took a temp job in a warehouse less than a mile from my home in South Yorkshire, England. Having responded to an advert in the local paper, I signed up with a dozen friends on the promise of a steady summer income from a logistics outsourcing company that had been engaged by a high-street clothing retailer. By then I had already worked a number of part-time jobs, but entering the warehouse was my first encounter with a truly mass workplace in which every aspect of the work process has been organised before work even begins.

We were grouped onto lines of twelve, each with a supervisor whose primary role seemed to be ensuring that we maintained a fast enough pace (fast enough for what, we were never told) and who would report figures to a manager every hour. Dozens of lines filled the vast warehouse, seemingly arranged only by break rotation – fifteen minutes every four hours, during which we were not allowed to leave an area inside the building enclosed by a steel-fenced security perimeter. The work involved processing end-of-range clothing that had been sent from stores across the country, 'retagging' them with discount offers, and packing them up to be sent back without stealing anything. It was as simple as that. Yet the operation as a whole perplexed me. Little did I know I was witnessing an organisational mode of work and management that had been a hundred years in the making, and one that in the next fifteen years would be fundamentally trans-formed in ways that can hardly be comprehended by the unassuming word 'digitalisation'.

This is not the first time the future of work has been contested. Nor is it the first time there have been debates about whether new workplace technologies will be beneficial or injurious to workers. But what if this framing gives a false impression of the options available to us? What if there really is no chance that what we are witnessing unfold can actually be beneficial to workers? What if some new technologies are injurious not by chance but by design?

The archetypal example of a modern workplace where these concerns are at stake is the Amazon warehouse – or 'fulfilment centres', as the company calls them. In these facilities, poor employment protections, high workloads and advanced technology conspire to create high-turnover jobs that come with a harsh toll of mental and physical exhaustion. But such conditions are not confined to Amazon. They are widely acknowledged features of the so-called 'gig economy' as a whole, from transportation platforms like Uber and Lyft to food-delivery platforms such as Deliveroo in Britain or GrubHub in the United States. What unites the Deliveroo rider's app with the largest Amazon fulfilment centre is a shared technology. In this book I'm going to call it algorithmic management. It is a simple idea with big implications, made possible by the vast computational power now available to rich companies. Algorithmic management refers to a way of organising work in which workers are directed, monitored, tracked and assessed – all at once, in real time – by a computer system that doesn't rely on a human manager to control it. Far beyond its application in headline-grabbing companies such as Amazon, it is a way of organising work with wide-ranging consequences.

But aren't robots coming for our jobs? Beyond the PR of the wealthiest companies that can afford the most self-aggrandising research and development projects, this is generally not the case. I wouldn't be so foolish as to predict that unmanned delivery robots, Amazon drones and workerless 'lights-out' factories will *never* materialise, but for the moment the application of automation to work generally takes place in discrete sections of the work process – typically at the level of decision-making, rather than through the replacement of workers altogether. Aside from being costly to invent and acquire, robots need to be maintained, cleaned and fixed. Experiments with mobile robots in distribution warehouses quickly ran into the rather mundane problem of dust. While 'workerless' factories have been predicted since at least the 1970s, I would gently suggest we'll only really begin to see them in large numbers about a decade after companies master the 'dustless' warehouse. It's not impossible, but it's improbable. Even in the oft-cited example of the supermarket self-service checkout, it's not that the work of scanning has actually been automated – it has simply been transferred from a paid employee to the paying customer.

The fact is that, for most practical work, human workers are simply cheaper, more reliable and easier to replace than robots. Rather than being replaced by computers, it is instead the case that ever more workers are being managed by them, by virtue of workers being subject to algorithms – computational codes, or rules, that once executed convert data into decisions.

Just as a calculator (just one type of computing machine) can outstrip mental arithmetic, algorithms can do things that people simply cannot. They can draw on an extraordinary range of information, decide and act in real time, monitor and measure with a high degree of accuracy, close ambiguities, work constantly, interact with users dispassionately, and – if necessary – archive, or 'remember', everything. Within a work context, they can integrate a wide range of modular technologies (especially for tracking), connect physical actions to digital records, mediate between different types of information and make calculations of efficiency based on a range of variables. For a human this work is complex and time-consuming, if it is possible at all; for a computer system it is both quick and easily repeatable. Moreover, and not insignificantly, calculations produced by computers attract an air of infallibility or objectivity among human users. In the ideal algorithmic management form, replaceable workers work on the basis of algorithmic decisions, and are held to 'objective' standards set by algorithmic analytics.

This is the real future of automation.

This is a book about workers and algorithms. But, like most books about workers, it is really about power; and, like most meaningful reflections on algorithms, it is really about communication and control – which is to say, cybernetics. Cybernetics is an old term that in modern usage is best thought of as the science, study or conceptualisation of systems of communication and control. The most widely understood principle given to us by cybernetics is the idea of the feedback loop: a circuit or process in which some output is 'fed back' into a system as input, typically with the aim of correcting or optimising that system. For our purposes, what cybernetics is interested in is the ability to use feedback loops to control or steer a complex system (in this case, a workplace).

You do not need a technical knowledge of computers, software or code to read this book. It will be enough merely to have some idea that computational technology now shapes our everyday experience of the world in extensive ways, from smartphones and the screens that are becoming ubiquitous in public spaces to Bluetooth and barcodes. Similarly, you do not need to have ever worked with an algorithm, though the chances are you already have, knowingly or not. It is enough that you have an interest in workers and their working lives, and care what the future holds for them – for us.

So workers are being managed by computers rather than replaced by them, and those computers are organised on the basis of cybernetic feedback loops that control or steer the workplace. Can workers fight back? The answer to that is not straightforward.

In the Anglophone world, trade unions have been the primary vehicle of working-class power for at least the last hundred years. There are trade unions for almost every line of work we can imagine, and an increasing number of general unions that cast a wide net over lots of different types of workplace, particularly those in the private sector. Within the political and economic system in which we live – capitalism – trade unions are basically a good thing. They mediate between labour (workers) and the forces of capital (employers, owners and, where necessary, government), and they are largely responsible for working norms like paid annual leave, the five-day week, the eight-hour day, child labour laws, and health and safety legislation. Yet trade unions are not the same as working-class power, especially in the context of algorithmic management.

In the contemporary economy, there is no doubt that unions continue to be valuable, and it is true that, in both Britain and the United States, the trade union movement has been beset by the repressive and hateful anti-union agendas of successive governments since at least the 1980s. I make no concession to such laws, which are designed to stifle the ability of working-class people to express themselves politically within the world of work. But there should be no doubt that there are better and worse unions in terms of ambition, strategy and political will, and that within even the most impressive unions there are both proactive and reactionary factions, as anyone who has ever participated in union organising can attest.

But where technology is concerned, trade unions remain on the back foot, even without the assistance of the political opponents of the working class. Or, perhaps more generously, the distance trade unions have to cover to meet the demands of the present moment depends on their historical relationship to questions concerning technology and the work process. Yet the continued application of digital technology to work, and workers more generally, is a future we are all going to be forced to confront one way or another. In this book we will encounter a number of workplaces where this is already happening, and I will use those cases to explain what is at stake in the digital future of work, and why, whether we like it or not, we are forced either to change our approach or accept a future in which workers' health, happiness and freedom are readily sacrificed in the name of optimisation, performance and profit. I am in no doubt that the stakes are this high. However, I wish to be clear from the outset that any criticisms of trade unions presented in this book arise solely from a desire to see workers on the front foot in the fight for better work and a better society. Moreover, any such criticisms should be understood as being levelled at political directions, modes and stances rather than at individuals or unions themselves.

I am writing this book because in a world where the vast majority of us are compelled to work in order to live, the future of work matters – which is to say: workers matter. It matters whether people spend half their waking lives happy or stressed; it matters whether we feel ourselves to be dehumanised or dignified; it matters whether workers are powerless, or – as the case may be – not. This means the conditions that organise our work should always be a political priority, at least as long as life and society are organised around work in turn.

Algorithms are now the lifeblood of industrial innovation, and algorithmic management represents a precipice from which we will struggle to return if we do not take it seriously. Unfortunately, so-called 'human-centred' approaches to this problem offer little in this regard. Humans – and, more significantly, politics – are already at the centre of the algorithm. Nor is there any amount of job security or mending wages that will mitigate algorithmic management itself. What we need, therefore, is a political understanding of algorithmic management on its own terms. The task of interrogating workplace technologies should be fixated less on what can be done to make them 'fairer' within parameters acceptable to the parties implementing them – a paternalistic, conservative posture that is too often adopted uncritically – and more engaged with the questions of power that led to injurious technologies being introduced into workplaces (itself a euphemism – we ought to say *imposed upon workers*) in the first place. This means starting with algorithmic management as we find it.

By necessity, where there are workers, there is also politics. Workers are variously unpredictable, fallible, collaborative, creative, lazy, cooperative, uncooperative and much else besides. In a word, they are free, and by their most basic and human capacity for autonomy introduce uncertainty into a finely calibrated calculus for making money. If one of the applications of digital technology to work and workers is the reduction of this uncertainty, it is a fundamentally political set of concerns – ones not merely reducible to their economic rationale – that is at stake in algorithmic management and the digitalisation of the workplace.

A non-exhaustive list of workplaces where algorithmic management technologies are now being deployed includes factories, courts, newsrooms, cafés, restaurants, taxi firms, courier services, creative suites, offices, care providers and call centres. At the apex are logistical workplaces, which constitute a pathfinder sector. For this reason, I will focus here on workplaces along the logistical supply chain, though the lessons they offer will be pertinent elsewhere. Although Amazon warehouses are the archetypal algorithmic workplace, uncovering the politics of algorithmic management will also require us to look more closely at workplaces that usually elude the headlines, in order to see how algorithmic workplaces operate and how workers might apply political agency within them. What such workplaces have in common with Amazon is that they are generally hard to access, and the managerial forms that dominate them are often characterised as both omnipotent and opaque. I wish to advance an alternative view.

Owing to the decades-long assault on wages and employment security, the common starting point for thinking about algorithmic workplaces tends to be 'precarity' – an 'ugly neologism', as Mark Fisher put it: the observation that insecure work leads workers into increasingly insecure lives. This is a worthy cause, but in my view it does not get us very far in understanding the political stakes of algorithms at work. As such, I want to foreground what in the past has been considered a 'deeper unrest' within the workplace. Over a hundred years ago, at the beginning of his 1921 thesis *The Frontier of Control*, Carter L. Goodrich quoted William Straker, the general secretary of the Northumberland Miners' Association, in an address to a Coal Commission meeting at the House of Lords:

> In the past workmen have thought that if they could secure higher wages and better conditions they would be content. Employers have thought that if they granted these things the workers ought to be contented. Wages and conditions have been improved; but the discontent and the unrest have not disappeared ... Many good people have come to the conclusion that working people are so unreasonable that it is useless trying to satisfy them. The fact is that the unrest is deeper than pounds, shillings and pence, necessary as they are. The root of the matter is the straining of the spirit of man to be free.[1]

Straker's words are evocative and invigorating, but Goodrich found them useful for distinguishing 'the unrest which is concerned more with discipline and management than with wages'. This is a distinction that can serve us well today, reminding us that there is more at stake in the future of work than remuneration and certainty. Goodrich described this other side of work, and its discontent, under the rubric of *control*. It's a term he chose precisely because of its messiness and malleability, representing a diverse range of rights, claims and motives on the part of both employers and workers. In doing so, he identified a contested threshold running through the workplace: the 'frontier of control', or the point at which the employer aims to say: 'Beyond this there shall be no discussion, the rest is my business alone', against which workers might test the limits of their ability to control or shape their own work environment.[2]

I want to change the way we think about digital technologies at work. Rather than seeing the rise of algorithmic management as part of a general 'spread of automation' and a natural step in the trajectory of computerisation, I want us to question what the stakes are for workers and work, and what it means for technologies of control and communication to be sites of struggle and contestation. In short, I want to elevate the idea that, to understand what digitalisation means for the present and future of work, we need to account for *algorithmic power* as a mode of politics not reducible to what we think we know about the struggle between workers and bosses.

Of course, questions of technology have always included issues of workplace politics; yet for too long we have been on the back foot in relation to them. In 1949, the cybernetician Norbert Wiener tried to persuade Walter Reuther, the head of United Auto Workers, either to make cybernetic technologies the union's business or else campaign for their suppression.[3] A year later, Reuther signed the landmark Treaty of Detroit with General Motors, a five-year deal that would set norms of industrial relations in the motor industry and in many other sectors for decades to come. In the Treaty, the union staked a claim on pay, pensions and holidays on the explicit understanding that it would jettison any claim to 'corporate decision-making', including the labour process and the use of technology, instead recognising the company's 'right to manage' as its business alone. This is a norm still upheld by trade unions the world over.

Digital technologies have by now become part of the fabric of everyday life, and in many ways the introduction of algorithmic techniques to workplaces seems somewhat unremarkable, or even inevitable.[4] Yet it is precisely for this reason that workplace technology must now be repoliticised, after decades in the hands of bosses. As supermarket worker Adam Barr has observed, working alongside a technology that seems opaque and pervasive can give the impression of the suppression of politics altogether, let alone political possibility.[5] And yet we can draw hope from the fact that, in the words of Mark Fisher, 'The very oppressive pervasiveness of capitalist realism means that even glimmers of alternative political and economic possibilities can have a disproportionately great effect.'[6]

This book advocates a project of identifying such glimmers – events which might tear small holes in the curtain of algorithmic management, indicating new avenues for workers to advance upon the workplace claims of their own, and expanding the horizons of possibility beyond what was previously presumed to be its frontier.

2

Algorithmic Work

*Only by understanding the actual conditions of life
and the actual strivings of an actual working class
at a certain stage of its development, can the problems of humanity as a whole be understood.*
— Ria Stone, *The American Worker*

It was in a supermarket that most people began to
understand the gravity of the Covid-19 pandemic.
Almost overnight, shoppers found themselves navigating sanitised trolleys between the zealous
moralism about 'panic buying' and the reality of
shelves emptying faster than they could be replen-
ished. While scuffles over basic goods were more
likely to be seen on social media than in person, the
folk devil of the 'greedy shopper' was a useful dis-
traction from a more fundamental problem: that
the organisation of supermarket logistics was sud-
denly unable to ensure that supply followed demand.[1]

The moralism was backed up by an emerging
mantra: 'Take only what you need and there will be
enough for everyone.' Mark Price, former managing
director of the British supermarket chain Waitrose,
said in March 2020:

> The supply of goods, the manufacture of food, is in
> good shape. There isn't a problem there; there is

enough food ... The challenge that the supermarkets are facing at the moment is getting that food into their distribution centres and then having enough space, and having enough lorries and drivers to get it to the shops, and then being able to keep it on the shelves.[2]

In reality, this challenge spoke less to the behaviour of individual shoppers, selfish or otherwise, than to the nature of the logistics that supermarkets rely upon. It might have been comforting to know enough food existed – and that, in an abstract sense, there would be enough to go around – but it meant little if supermarkets couldn't get it onto their own shelves.

Few logistical infrastructures can claim to be more enmeshed with daily life than supermarkets. By now, major supermarkets are experts in the business of efficient purchasing, storage and predictive analytics. Even the most obscure non-perishable item rarely sits on a shelf long enough to gather dust. In one famous instance, following Hurricane Katrina's battering of Louisiana in August 2005, Walmart was able to mobilise its logistical systems to provide essential items to thousands of affected people on a non-commercial basis more speedily than the National Guard.

We might ask, then, why supermarket supply chains – the logistical networks responsible for getting products into distribution centres and out onto shelves – were not better equipped to reorient themselves towards the set of demands placed on them by the onset of the pandemic. The answer is that a national lockdown forced us all to think, shop and act in very similar ways within the same short period of time. With the best will in the world, supermarkets do not stock enough units of essential goods for each household to buy even one handwash, toilet roll and bag of flour at the same time. Generally, that isn't how people shop, and the regime of predictive analytics means that if people do not usually shop a certain way, then supermarkets won't automatically prepare for it. Of course, supermarkets are used to making seasonal adjustments, most notably at Christmas, when thousands of extra staff are hired both in-store and across the entire supply chain – but such an operation typically necessitates a four-month build-up period.

All logistics, then, involves decisions – or calculations – about how goods and labour will move across time and space. But the principal idea governing contemporary logistics is to minimise 'waste'. By minimising waste, in the broadest sense, you maximise efficiency (and therefore profit) through the reduction of as much surplus time and space as possible. Classically, this means an aversion to large warehouses with expensive ground rent filled with stock for longer than is absolutely necessary. Instead, dynamic distribution hubs are used, with 'fulfilment centres' where stock turnover is very high and flows of inbound and outbound goods are constant. In a system with high demand but generally little in the way of stored stock, these logistics hubs rely on well-calibrated linkages across the supply chain. This generally involves a combination of algorithmic inventory and order management with deskilled, replaceable and often poorly paid workers who can be swapped in and out easily. The essential principle is that goods are moved between each stage of the supply chain just in time to meet demand, and not before – hence this system is known as 'just-in-time' logistics.

As much as anything else, though, supply chains depend on logistics workers. It doesn't matter how much food you have queueing up to get to a distribution centre if you haven't got enough healthy staff to sort it and distribute it, and you don't have enough lorry drivers to run deliveries of every item to every store each day.

Yet within the just-in-time management philosophy – and it is a philosophy – the labour force is also regarded as a form of waste to be minimised. Every effort is made to ensure that workers are as productive as humanly possible: think of the till operators in a budget supermarket rushing to meet scanning targets on pain of disciplinary measures. Further along the supply chain in distribution centres, as we will see, it is common for supermarket deliveries to be organised by outsourced workers who are allocated shifts on the basis of text messages that tell them whether or not their daily performance has secured them another day's work. Within just-in-time logistics, time is always money. While it was always more convenient to blame consumer behaviour, as if a global health emergency wasn't going to make people head to the shops, it was in fact supermarkets' enduring obsession with efficiency and minimising 'waste' – including the workforce – that sabotaged their ability to fill their own shelves.

While the pandemic exposed a number of logistical frailties, it was also one of the rare periods in which we were able to see the cracks in what is usually a very smooth veneer. As the labour writer Kim Moody has noted, logistics is now the fastest-growing sector in the world, largely thanks to the growth of platform capitalism – the emergence of digital platforms as economic intermediaries – and e-commerce.[3] It may seem ironic that the digital economy is underpinned by such physical processes, but it shouldn't be surprising: the entire internet, of course, is itself made possible by a practical infrastructure of cables, servers and data centres involving all manner of manual and technical labour.

Yet as the digital economy has cemented itself as a normal part of everyday life, the technology-driven work practices that underpin it have attracted scrutiny. In Britain, the words 'Sports Direct' – the name of a notorious e-commerce retailer – have become synonymous with poor working conditions in the popular imagination. Meanwhile, the distribution warehouses behind e-commerce sites such as Amazon and Asos have been subject to investigations into their operation of algorithmic management techniques – particularly the use and abuse of stringent productivity targets and surveillance.[4] In response, legislators have attempted to grapple with the concerns surrounding algorithmically managed work by questioning the working conditions at distribution warehouses, courier delivery services and high-profile 'gig economy' companies, albeit to little effect.

The confluence of technological changes and employment insecurity has been widely observed by the labour movement in recent years, both in

Britain and internationally. Beneath the veneer of flexibility and autonomy lies the use of technology to facilitate bogus forms of 'self-employment' without either employment rights or the autonomy possessed by genuine freelancers or sole traders: the use of apps to penalise workers who turn down work assigned to them; aggressive surveillance and tracking; and productivity regimes in e-commerce warehouses so stringent that, in one notorious case, workers felt forced to urinate in bottles rather than walk to the toilet.

It's little surprise, then, that research on algorithmic management quickly arrived at the question of whether digitalised work could be made more humane.[5] The hunch was that improvements around transparency and optimisation might be the key to putting 'humans at the centre of the algorithm': initial ideas included introducing some degree of transparency over algorithmic decision-making, data-gathering and the setting of targets; or the optimisation of the way decisions over groups of workers are calculated to incorporate values such as equity and fairness, rather than being organised through a coldly mathematical approach. The jury is still out on this, but it is notable that such concerns were raised almost from the moment of the adoption of algorithmic management – and, more worryingly still, that it is one of the first priorities to be dropped when the rubber meets the road for concerned parties campaigning for improvements in the sector.

On a cool morning in April 2013, over a thousand trade unionists armed with whistles and high-vis vests formed a picket line outside an Amazon distribution centre in Bad Hersfeld, central Germany. The action began a campaign of walkouts which, by 2016, would cost over a hundred workdays, and marked the first ever strike against the e-commerce, entertainment and digital services giant. Facilitated by the Ver.di general union, the campaign was notable both for being the first of its kind, and for its industrial, proactive character in the face of a belligerent of immense power; Amazon having already crushed trade union ambitions for a decade in Britain by that time.[6] In the decade since 2013, union activities against Amazon have only grown worldwide, including in the United States, where an embattled union drive in Alabama spurred activists on to achieving recognition – at least notionally – for a union branch for New York Amazon workers in 2022.

Foremost among Ver.di's objectives was a collective agreement between the union and the employer, a demand echoed by unions across the logistics sector internationally, the rationale being to link union recognition and representation with protections for workers, specifically in terms of wages and conditions. Such demands usually face anti-union tactics, either overt or implicit. In Spain and Italy, union campaigns against logistics companies were met with police violence. In Britain, unions have had to deal with a lack of access to workers and workplaces, a workforce divided between employment agencies, employers signing sweetheart deals with so-called 'moderate' unions to undermine their campaigning counterparts, and ambivalence on the part of the political wing of the labour movement, which has expressed concern over working conditions in the sector while subsidising companies like

Amazon on the promise of bringing jobs to deindustrialised areas.

Amazon is a 'laboratory of resistance'.[7] It's a metaphor that gives a sense of the trials of the labour movement, which has, over the past decade, attempted to grapple with a broad, entangled knot comprising the emerging working practices and conditions symbolised by Amazon on one hand, and the working conditions of the so-called gig economy on the other.

The new world of work, with Amazon at its heart, has been met by labour and social movements in various ways. The industrial action against Amazon soon spread beyond Germany to fulfilment centres in Spain, Italy and Poland, before energising a handful of high-profile campaigns in the United States, and later in Britain. Meanwhile, the gig economy has seen its first 'strikes' by food platform workers against Deliveroo, Foodora and Uber Eats – as well as 'ride-sharers' against Uber – subverting the companies' insistence that their service providers are independent workers (rather than employees) by staging organised 'wildcat' actions in which workers simply agree not to log into their work apps. In response to the increasingly logistical character of the organisation of global capitalism, social movement actors have focused their energies on 'blocking' supply chains through occupations and blockades.[8] Meanwhile, trade unions in Britain have launched campaigns and legal challenges over working conditions in the 'digital economy'.[9] Historically, trade union campaigns – and their demands – have been primarily concerned with the principle of recognition, followed by pay and employment security. But while employment security is certainly important to workers' interests, and arguably their ability to act collectively, technological innovation has seldom registered highly among the priorities of the organised labour movement, despite the fact it is profoundly changing the social and political dynamics of the workplace.

Since 2020, when the pandemic put a fresh spotlight onto Amazon's working practices and the #MakeAmazonPay campaign was launched to coincide with Black Friday, unions began to look more closely at the regime of data tracking and AI surveillance that exists at Amazon and other algorithmically enabled employers.[10] Initially, this was confined to concerns about workplace health and safety – a well-trodden, if rather narrow, avenue for unions to assert themselves. More recently, however, union researchers have sought to break ground in the realm of digital rights, data processing and the application of artificial intelligence.

In Britain, official efforts around Amazon's use of algorithmic management are being guided by the TUC's *AI Manifesto*. Produced in 2021, the document calls for new legal protections in a context where employment law has fallen behind the curve on the use of digital technology at work. Its recommendations include a new right to 'human review', the establishment of 'employment-focused ethical principles' and a 'duty to consult' unions in relation to the deployment of AI in workplaces in which automated decision-making is deemed to present a high risk.

These recommendations rest on the imperative of making algorithmic decisions more 'transparent' or 'explainable'. But the idea that algorithmic transparency will make work more equitable, less stressful and safer is based on a misplaced sense that exposing the least visible part of a digital system – 'black-boxed' from view – will reveal to us the hidden elements that make working for Amazon so miserable. While it is good that unions are thinking about digital technology, by pinning any hopes of political advancement on data transparency they risk missing the point: it is a technical solution to a political problem. Transparency itself does not mean that what we find beneath the digital hood will help us navigate – and change – the power differentials between worker and company. There is simply no algorithm or section of code we could hope to isolate that would yield the explanatory power to account for the modes of organisation and politics we see enacted at Amazon.

But it is important not to disappear into the abstract. Because the politics of algorithmic management is so intimately entwined with the organisation of work, it is necessary to show how such workplaces function in practice – not least because their operation is typically hidden and highly securitised. As logistical workers in particular will attest, these are workplaces where phones are not allowed on shop floors, workers have to enter through security turnstiles, and digital ID access cards are becoming ever more normalised. Some workplaces even have random body searches, while all have a high degree of CCTV surveillance. While the complexity of class formation cannot be described merely in terms of the experience of particular workplaces, this should not prevent us from rooting our understanding of it within an engagement with actual work and the experiences of workers themselves. Too often, adherence to an avowedly 'structural' analysis simply masks a lack of engagement with the conditions of work in all their specificity and contingency. Logistical capitalism succeeds precisely because it is able to integrate the small-scale activities with the largest possible operations. Our thinking about it should be similarly ambitious.

In Yorkshire, there is a giant distribution centre whose three storeys cover an area the size of five football pitches.[11] Inside it, clothes are stacked on huge pallets and sorted into packages that are shipped out to thousands of homes around the world, packed by locally employed workers. The warehouse sits on part of the land formerly occupied by a colliery, just one among the dozens of sites of the year-long miners' strike of 1984–5. Once a mining stronghold, the pit was closed in 1993, and has since suffered from the damaging effects of deindustrialisation. It's a familiar story: many other former mines in the area are now crowned by logistics hubs, call centres and small out-of-town retail parks, owing to their pre-established transport connections and the ready availability of cheap labour from nearby towns.

The e-commerce company served by the distribution centre was a big winner from the dot-com boom of the early 2000s, and in recent years has attracted the attention of press and legislators alike over its working practices. The retail website from which the clothes are bought by consumers – the only part of the company that the public is likely to see – is an umbrella company. It handles marketing and purchases by customers, but the fulfilment of orders at the distribution centre is overseen by a different firm altogether, an American multinational logistics company that runs the warehouse and oversees its staffing.

In the regional office of a large general union I meet Elaine, an organiser who has been running a campaign around conditions at the site – though almost entirely from outside the warehouse gates, because the company has denied her access. Around half the staff at the warehouse are employed by an agency, Elaine estimates, with the other half employed directly by the logistics company. Employees of the logistics company are on 'flex' contracts, meaning that their working hours might be extended or reduced depending on company needs, but they remain paid at a constant wage rate. In the past, this arrangement often put workers in a difficult situation. Some reported learning through text messages that their shift had been delayed, shortened or extended once they were already on the bus into work – or even while on the job. As a result, workers often had to wait in the staff room, unpaid, before being allowed to start. In the case of unplanned extensions, this made life particularly difficult for those with caring responsibilities. When I speak to Elaine, workers are being given twenty-four hours' notice of their shift times following an initiative by the trade union – despite the union not being recognised by the company.

The company's level of trust in its employees is low. When they arrive onsite, all workers pass through security checks. The basic check involves guards using security wands, but workers also press a 'randomiser' button, which assigns workers to one of two levels of more detailed search. Inside the warehouse, stock from HGV loading bays is unpacked and sorted for storage at a rate of sixty-five items per hour. Workers further along the process are given a 'gun' (also known as a 'controller'), which houses a barcode scanner, a digital display and a wrist strap. The device tells the employee what to pick and where to find it. The pick line is laid out in what is described as a 'snake' (Elaine signs an 'S' shape), which is designed to prevent congestion – in principle, workers are to start at one end and come out at the other, repeating this same route throughout their shift.

The 'gun' also records the employee's pick rate, displaying a number. Elaine tells me the target is typically 185 items per hour, but this can fluctuate depending on the number of orders being placed online. There is no upper limit to the target. Workers' average pick rates are calculated for the whole time they are clocked in, including toilet breaks. 'Downtime' – the length of time between picks – is monitored by supervisors via the handset, and they use pick-rate and downtime data to discipline workers who fail to reach their targets.

Of course, the use of computerisation in logistics is nothing new, but here we can see how the assignment, administration, measurement and assessment of work by algorithms takes place in real time. Algorithms cover the allocation of work, the direction of the employee towards particular items, the employee's performance against a pick rate (itself set by the algorithm according to online order traffic), and the direction of supervisors towards workers who fail to meet targets. In such cases, algorithmic tracking and decision-making are either augmenting or replacing the traditional managerial or supervisory function, with workers directed by software based on real-time data processing.

This is algorithmic management, and we can already begin to see why it is such tricky ground for unions. Unions have a long-established protocol of maintaining a distance from the specific technologies adopted by employers in the pursuit of profit – as long as they are not being used to lay off workers, which in this case they are not. This position was characterised in 1964 by the Italian Marxist Raniero Panzieri as 'objectivist'. It upholds the idea that there is an 'objectivity' about the development and use of machinery, even if we might disagree with the economic context in which it is applied (namely, capitalist industry). This attitude is not confined to trade unions: it was shared by economistic forms of Marxism throughout the twentieth century, and persists today. What is needed instead is a more political orientation towards the development and use of technology. Whereas Panzieri's account occurred in what was still the age of machinery, when it was still possible to argue that machines could be configured for the worker's benefit, in the age of algorithms the question is instead whether workers can be configured for the benefit of the machine. This isn't merely an abstract question of the philosophy of technology: a real-world historical aversion to making demands about the application of technology in the productive process is now coming to bite, as digital technology is increasingly applied directly to the management of workers. As the sociologist Phoebe Moore has put it, where once we might have imagined computers to be a tool at the disposal of workers, workers are now being transformed into tools at the disposal of computational systems.[12]

The on-demand economy's ability to move products from a warehouse to the customer depends on a complicated logistical infrastructure. The day-to-day operation of logistics comprises warehouse pickers, packers, supervisors, drivers, riders and many other types of worker. These workers may be employees, agency workers, temporary staff or 'independent'. Logistics refers to *organisation* – the organisation of workers and workplaces to enable the movement of goods. But it also refers to *information*, and goods, workplaces and workers being understood as information. Logistical operations in this sense are a continuous process facilitated by digital technology and executed by algorithms. In other words, the fact that consumers can order groceries, clothes, books or hot meals to their door depends on a technical infrastructure of computers, devices and scanners that are joined both to goods in a supply chain and to workers in workplaces by software – code – that processes inputs and decides outputs in real time. These outputs move goods through space and, importantly, organise workers in their work.

This is a process that has been mastered by supermarkets, whose business model relies on the bulk-purchasing of goods, their effective distribution across stores and their sale to customers – all with minimal waste and warehousing. Given the almost mind-blowing scale and complexity of such operations, it is little wonder that many supermarket companies have successfully branched off into home delivery, or that stores that initially resisted developing their own last-mile delivery services are now partnering with delivery platforms like Gopuff.

North-east of London's largest airport lies the Heathrow service area. Made up of miles of housing estates, this area is home to large numbers of migrant workers and is dotted with warehouses and logistics hubs. Logistics is the primary industry in this corridor of Greater London, where goods are serviced as they arrive or depart from the airport, and the roads give off the crunching sounds of articulated lorries twenty-four hours a day. It is here that I meet Lorenzo, a European migrant who was, until recently, an agency-employed 'picker-packer' at a large food-distribution centre nearby. Walking through the industrial estate to what appears to be the only local pub, he points to the anonymous steel buildings lining the streets, describing the work that takes place inside each of them. Some are light industrial workplaces, many involved in food manufacturing. Most, however, are distribution centres. Lorenzo and others he knows who work locally have all rotated through many of these warehouses, which is typical of the local work culture. On the day I visit, I notice that the tiny convenience store by the train station stocks no fewer than twenty different brands of energy drink, each with multiple flavours, in an enormous fridge by the door.

Lorenzo's workplace is run by a logistics company but contracted by a national supermarket chain to sort and send food to stores across London around the clock. After arriving at the warehouse, employees receive a special 'watch' they use to clock in by scanning a barcode. The entire day's work will be governed by interaction with the watch – in fact a Motorola WT4000 device, more like a large, bulky smartphone strapped to the forearm than a wristwatch – and the activities of each watch are linked to an individual employee. Lorenzo is only paid for the time he is clocked in via the device.

Once employees are inside, they are directed to either the 'chilled' or 'produce' section. Both are cold: a working environment Lorenzo describes as 'hostile'. The chilled section is kept between 0°C and 2°C, the produce section at around 10°C. The shift's work takes place on one of six 'grids', each about 100 metres in length and designated by a certain type of goods. Working in 'produce' often involves carrying large boxes of vegetables, whereas 'small items' often involves packing sandwiches and yoghurts. Lorenzo tells me the division of produce often tends to inspire a gendered division among workers. In the first instance, men tend to take on heavier work, but Lorenzo notes that some workers try to enforce a 'men only' rule in the meat grid, seemingly with little regard for the actual physicality involved in the work.

Each shift is made up of 'assignments', each of which involves being allocated a pallet, scanning it, moving it using your assigned trolley, and then unloading items from the pallet into the cages along your grid. Once the cages are full, picker-packers are required to bring new cages to the grid, for which they are given a set amount of time. While working on the grid, time is of the essence: each assignment has a target productivity rate, measured by the pace at which items are scanned. Pallets can contain anything from one large item to 500 small items, and can often weigh around 600 or 700 kilograms. Sometimes, although a pallet is physically ready, it cannot be electronically received by the picker-packer because it has not been registered into the database, slowing the worker's productivity rate. As we will see later, this is the rate against which workers are awarded shifts.

Each of the packers' watches contains a screen interface, a number pad and a barcode scanner that is clipped onto the end of the index finger to enable workers to handle and scan items simultaneously. Once workers have a pallet, the watch will tell them where to go (to which cage) and which items to transfer. Both the cage and the item must be scanned each time, and receipt of the item must be confirmed using the buttons. 'The watch is sort of heavy,' Lorenzo says. 'It's like 400 grams or something. Which doesn't seem too much, but if you've got 200 items per hour, that's like 1,600 per shift, and for each item you have to look at it. So you make this kind of hand movement about 4,000 times.'

Through the scanning of items, managers compile records of workers' productivity rates both per assignment (pallet) and across their shift. Two main figures are communicated to workers: a percentage based on the company's hourly pick targets, and a cases-per-minute (CPM) rate. Lorenzo describes various ways for workers to be informed of their productivity rate throughout each shift: 'A supervisor of the temp agency – this doesn't apply for the permanent workers – comes along and picks out people who are too slow and they show them a printout which shows up to the last half hour what your pick rate was, and if it's, let's say, below 90 per cent, they will say you have to work harder. Another way is a screen inside the warehouse. At one end of the grid, you can see your own code and the percentage. The problem they have with that is that workers [laughs] were standing there for about five minutes to wait for their number to come up, and they always had a commotion in front of these screens, so after six months they abolished them. They said health and safety, but later they were switched on again. It was like in the airport where you wait for your number to come up – but they have like ten codes on there and there are eighty people.'

Workers are released for their break in groups of ten, often causing delays. There can also be delays of up to an hour at the end of a shift, Lorenzo says, as workers are required to stay until their pallets are finished. At the end of the day, workers scan off the grid and clock out, ending their paid time, and return the watch to a supervisor.

The goods that workers spend their days sorting are organised into deliveries for individual supermarket locations – including both large superstores and smaller convenience stores – and pre-categorised by workers according to both item location or type, and stock replenishment needs. Superstores in particular now have a dual function: they are both physical spaces used by customers and also de facto warehouses for workers in online shopping departments. This is an industry that, despite an initially slow uptake following its launch in the late 1990s is now booming, claiming around 15 per cent of the market in Britain.

Todd is a young graduate who lives in a busy town on the south coast of England. Over lunch, we meet in a pub that seems to play only eighties rock music. It's midday, but Todd has already been awake for many hours. He has spent the morning working as a 'shopper' for an online shopping department at a major supermarket. Based in a normal store that is closed from 11 p.m. to 7 a.m., he begins work at 4 a.m. and finishes at 10 a.m. His job is to collect items from shelves which will then be collated into full shopping orders in the rear-of-house loading area, ready to be delivered to customers' homes.

When Todd arrives at work, he attends a team meeting in the empty loading area, where various pieces of information will be relayed to staff – usually either the results of 'secret shoppers' (people sent into stores to check whether employees are adhering to customer service rules) or a motivational talk from a manager. Todd then takes a handheld scanner from a shelf and logs himself in. He is then assigned a 'shop' – an algorithmically sorted assignment – and a starting point, to which he takes a special trolley that holds eight boxes. Each of the boxes corresponds to an individual customer, but generally Todd will not collect a customer's entire order. Instead, for each shop, he will pick a portion of eight individual orders, with full orders compiled only after he has taken the trolley to the loading area. The rationale is waste reduction: instead of having Todd and his colleagues all navigating the entire store to pick a single customer's mix of fresh food, cupboard items, bottles, frozen food, cleaning products, toiletries, and so on, workers can remain in one area of the store, reducing travelling time between areas.

The screen on Todd's handheld scanner shows him a single item at a time, along with its precise location. After each item is picked, the next-closest item by distance will be shown. If an item is in its correct location, it is Todd's responsibility to find it. In the case of an item that is sold out, he makes an appropriate substitution. After scanning an item, the screen will tell Todd where to place it on the trolley; the rear-of-house workers rely on the precise trolley location of individual items when they compile the full delivery orders. It used to be the case that one of Todd's trolleys might fill up before the shop had finished, but since the introduction of a new system, products are now pre-weighed and measured, and shops are calculated to incorporate the spatial requirements for transporting the products on the trolley. If there is not enough room in a box for the specified product, Todd presses an 'item will not fit' button, which will cancel from the shop any comparable or larger items which had been intended for that particular box.

Once the trolley is full, Todd takes it to the loading area. Here, boxes known as totes are put in rows to be loaded into vans. Once the shift is underway, this is a busy area. While there are anywhere between twenty and forty shoppers on shift at any one time (as well as a full team of shelvers), there are generally only five or six team members sorting boxes for the roughly twelve vans, and even fewer loading them. Supervision is carried out by two shop-side team leaders, a manager for the tote sorters, a manager and team leader for the vans, two overall managers, and the head of the store. Store security begins at 7 or 8 a.m.

Todd's performance is measured based on items picked per hour (IPH). His target used to be 115, but since the new system was brought in it has increased to 125. This new system has led to more densely packed, and therefore heavier, trolleys. Where once a particularly large shop would be around 120 items, and normal shops would often have half-full boxes, now it is 'not uncommon to see a 200-item shop where literally the whole box will be full up'. There is nothing on Todd's scanner to tell him whether he is reaching his target, but team leaders have access to live IPHs on a computer and will usually tell workers if they are not performing as required.

At the end of a shift it is common for team leaders to ask shoppers to stay on longer if they are part-way through a shop, but with the new system it is becoming more typical for them to finish before the shift is over, in which case they are asked to help the shelving team.

While some supermarkets are now integrating with gig economy platforms like Gopuff, which is designed for smaller shops and advertises a limited selection of products, the bulk of online supermarket shopping is delivered in specialist refrigerated vehicles operated by the supermarket itself. Deliveries are made from early in the morning until late at night, depending on slots pre-booked by customers when they place their order.

A short while after our interview about the distribution centre, I receive an email from Lorenzo telling me he is now working as a driver for a large supermarket chain, home-delivering grocery shopping bought online, and we agree to meet again to discuss his work.

There are two types of distribution centre where orders are fulfilled before being loaded for delivery, he tells me: superstores, with 'shoppers' who pick customers' items from normal supermarket shelves – the kind where Todd works – and specialised warehouses, which are not open to the public. Lorenzo works at the second type. At his workplace there are around 1,400 workers, he says, including around 600 drivers, though not all work at the same time – shoppers, in particular, often work only part-time. Lorenzo guesses there are around 200 shoppers in the warehouse at any given point. Around 50 per cent of the drivers, he estimates, are Black or Asian, mostly south Asian or Afro-Caribbean, and around 10 per cent are Eastern European. Drivers are generally employed as permanent staff, but some work through an agency. He observes that shoppers work with handheld devices up and down aisles, putting items into totes, much as described by Todd, except in this case conveyors take the items to the loading bay where loaders fill up the van sequentially. As a driver, Lorenzo collects the van from the yard after it is loaded; there are generally no mistakes in how the vans are filled, he says. Although he doesn't have an allocated delivery area, he is generally confined to the same geographical quarter of London, servicing the area within a fifteen-mile radius of the distribution centre.

Working in two four-hour blocks with a break in between, Lorenzo uses a handheld device like those used by postal workers and couriers. The device is as crucial to Lorenzo's work as the van. It incorporates a sat-nav, customer orders, a scanner and a mobile phone. There used to be multiple devices, he says, but workers requested an integrated machine. At the start of a delivery, he enters the customer's details into the sat-nav, and this gives him the route to the delivery site, providing traffic updates on the way. The sat-nav is 'intelligent', Lorenzo says: drivers are encouraged to take a 'better' route if they know one, which the sat-nav then learns for future use. This usually works, he says, although it occasionally creates problems with narrow carriageways, for example, that prevent access to large vehicles. In addition to the device, drivers have a paper manifest for use if the machine fails. Each four-hour block will generally take Lorenzo to between four and ten customers, up to a maximum of twenty in a full two-block shift.

Lorenzo generally follows the sat-nav to the customer's door, but he tells me that this can be difficult on built-up estates. Once the delivery is made, Lorenzo uses the scanner to take the customer's signature. If the customer is unhappy about an item, the scanner is also used to note the item and to credit the customer's online account. In cases where there is a delay with a delivery, a customer is not home, or there is balance still to pay on an order, the device can also be used as a phone to speak to a call centre – though Lorenzo tells me he uses his personal phone instead, as the device doesn't allow him to access customer details while he is on a call. Many drivers, he tells me, rely to a degree on their own phones, as Google Maps is better than the device's sat-nav. Generally, he carries the totes into the customer's kitchen for them; sometimes he tries to make conversation to pass the time.

After four hours he is expected to be back at the yard – but he is not expected to return before the four hours are up, even if he does not need the full amount of time to complete the orders. Sometimes productivity can be as low as three customers in four hours, in which case drivers will take longer breaks alone in the van. On other days, they struggle to finish inside the four hours. If drivers are left with spare time between deliveries, they are encouraged to call customers to see if they would like their delivery sooner; but as each customer has a delivery time-slot and drivers are not allowed to turn up early unannounced, and given the necessary time allowed for travel disruption, the schedule tends to be fairly generous. There is generally little time pressure on workers, he says – though the reception desk will use positive encouragement to try to get them to take an extra batch of orders in their van if there is a shortage of drivers and they have the room.

Drivers can refuse to take extra loads, but they will be paid overtime if it is required to complete orders. There are no penalties for being late, and the length of their breaks will not be affected. It took Lorenzo about a month to realise this, he tells me. Until then, he found the work quite stressful because he was always rushing to be on time while trying to get used to the sat-nav, as well as navigating unfamiliar parts of the city. Sometimes the work is still stressful – it's often physically demanding, and driving conditions can be poor – but it's often enjoyable, too. 'On a good day it's a bit of this, kind of, "masculine freedom",' he says. 'You're driving, you listen to some music, you drive through areas of London you haven't seen, you're going through some estates, there's a kind of easiness about it.' He also meets a wide range of customers, and says that he finds it interesting seeing how other people live and eat – although this can also be a mixed experience: sometimes, he says, it is as if you are assisting 'someone to commit suicide because basically they don't eat and just drink, and then you go to people with like three servants'. But customers form the main source of sociality: 'I never had a job where I talk less.'

While he is driving, he often speaks on the phone with friends, and sometimes chats to other drivers at the beginning or the end of shifts. But even after six months he only knows twenty or so of the 600 drivers. As for in-person supervision, he says he didn't see a human manager for the first three months, and was only introduced to one after he received a complaint from a customer about not being apologetic enough for running late with a delivery. Still, he is aware that his work record is kept on file: he says he once scratched a bus with his van, and he also had to have a return-to-work meeting after taking four days' sickness within six months ('That's over the 3 per cent mark'). But minor misdemeanours like lateness do not seem to be a big problem, as long as drivers call in to the call centre en route and, above all, do not leave the assigned route. While some deviations are permitted, workers are informed that their movements are monitored via the vehicle's GPS and front-facing CCTV, including things like speeding and sharp braking, which are measured using a telematics device in the van.

If modern logistics depends on computation, then at the heart of modern logistical organisation, architecture professor Jesse LeCavalier argues, is the ability to first turn objects into information.[13] It is not an accident that, in every workplace we have become acquainted with so far, the scanner has been the fundamental tool of the algorithmically mediated worker. In fact, the scanner has been the instrument that has enabled workers to become tools of the algorithmic system.

To understand how this happened, we need to consider an unassuming technology first used on a pack of Wrigley's Juicy Fruit chewing gum in Ohio in 1974 – a technology that went on to have enormous practical and theoretical consequences: the barcode. On a functional level, this seemingly banal innovation requires four initial components to work together in some sort of alignment: a graphic of thick and thin lines; an optical scanner capable of decoding the graphic; a database against which the code can be identified with a corresponding description or value; and a computer to process the data. The fifth component that ensures this configuration of elements has some desired effect is an algorithm: a sequence of operational instructions that tells the computer how to process the data. As we all know, a sixth component is typically added to this mix: a visual display (perhaps accompanied with an audible 'beep') to communicate to the user that the whole process has been executed with the desired effect.

The ability to scan barcodes on a pack of chewing gum saves the time, and therefore the labour, of the cashier – a modest automation of a repetitive task, like the manual entry of data at a till (or, further back, the writing of transactions in a ledger). This in turn increases the speed of the customer service, thereby minimising the number of cashiers required. This is commonly supplemented with a performance target, resulting in the often-observed process of cashiers at budget outlets throwing items towards a customer as fast as possible. Many shops have taken this principle a step further, and now encourage the customer to scan their own groceries – an innovation made possible by the integration of hardware and databases for measuring the weight of goods bought – in a move that reduces the staffing requirements of the retailer even as it precipitates a greater investment in security.

At an even more strategic level, however, a key value of barcode technology is that it facilitates an interaction between a physical product and a digital stock database. As goods are scanned when they are bought, the supermarket knows at all times the quantity of stock on shelves, minimising both the prospect of selling out unexpectedly or of buying too much stock. Coupled with the ability to analyse and compare data over time – and to combine it with other variables such as footfall, time of day, and the detailed customer intelligence provided by store loyalty cards – supermarkets now have the ability to plan their entire operation. This means that goods are less likely to linger on shelves unsold, while giving stores the ability to provide as many purchasable items as possible to match demand, all with minimal wasted cost.

As we can see, algorithms are crucial to the practical organisation of modern retail. The ability to pair items with a database, to scan products through individual tills, and to combine and process data in complex ways in real time enables supermarkets to achieve ever-greater levels of optimisation. Central to this effort is something called predictive analytics, which is the algorithmic analysis of data about past and current activities that can enable a business to plan to meet future needs as efficiently as possible, and to continuously improve the process in a feedback loop. It is no exaggeration to say that this entire system is practically a science for making money – and the supermarket industry understands it as such.

This would be reason enough to predict that digitalisation represents the future of work. But now consider that, under algorithmic management, workers too are reduced to information. We will arrive at the real implications of this in due course. But first let's consider a relatively recent use-case. It will not have escaped general notice that, since the Covid-19 pandemic, there has been an explosion in the use of 'quick response', or QR, codes – matrix bar codes that can contain more information than standard UPC barcodes. First created in the 1990s, QR codes have grown in use and popularity in recent years due to their easy readability, before becoming ubiquitous during the pandemic. As in many areas, Amazon was ahead of the curve. In March 2017, the company filed a patent for augmented reality goggles which could be worn by warehouse operatives to assist them in locating items and available shelf space within storage areas. The patent application described the goggles as combining both the scanning and instruction functions currently fulfilled by handheld scan guns with a locative system which uses location identifiers (imagined as QR codes) within the worker's field of vision to place them at any given moment, and to report when they have deviated from their instructed course (see Figures 1 and 2).[14]

When the patent application was published in August 2018, unions likened the idea to George Orwell's all-seeing Big Brother. But while the goggles would certainly assist managerial surveillance, this comparison missed the key point for prospective companies: to further the digital 'tooling' of human workers in service of the algorithmic system. It is not just that the goggles enable managers to see; they also subjugate workers' very presence within the workplace to production, transforming each worker into an embodied real-time data tracker. Although it is important to remember that a patent application is not the same thing as an invention, the designs are indicative of Amazon's intention to deepen its algorithmic management capability and to secure for itself every conceivable means of optimising its operation. In this case, replacing scan guns with goggles even manages to remove workers' basic ability to decide what gets

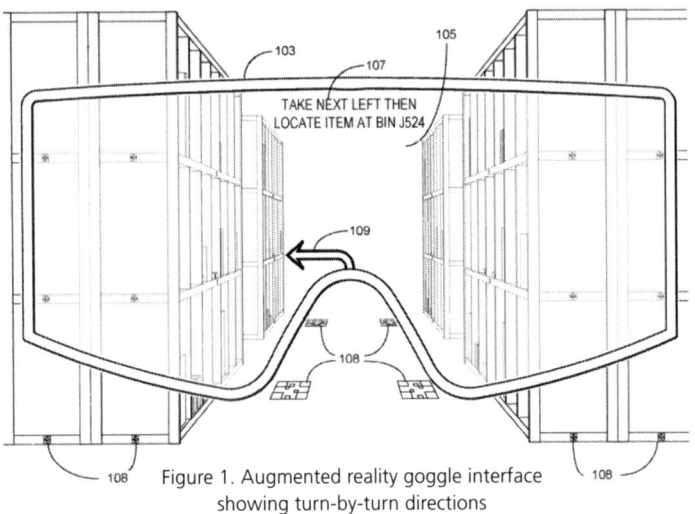

Figure 1. Augmented reality goggle interface
showing turn-by-turn directions

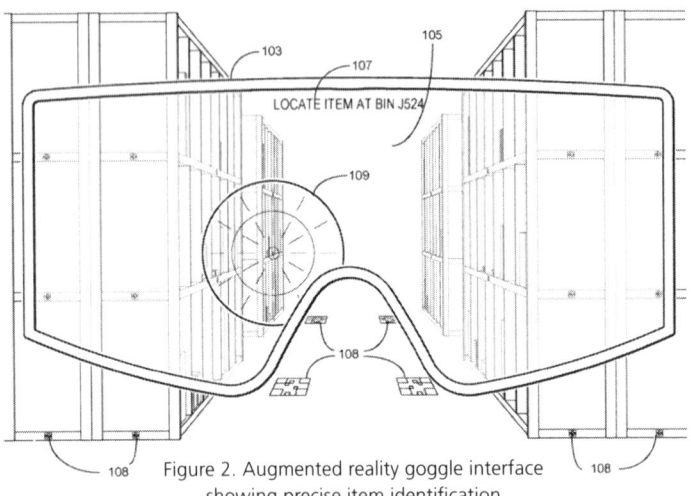

Figure 2. Augmented reality goggle interface
showing precise item identification

scanned or not; even when the wearer shuts their eyes, the goggles see all.

Work as a courier for Deliveroo, delivering food to the homes of eager customers, begins with a simple telephone interview and a basic induction with a 'lead rider'. The induction includes a gruelling test, in which potential riders are asked questions like, 'Do you wash your hands after you go to the toilet?' and 'You come to a red traffic light. Do you a) stop or b) go?' Respondents who fail can take unlimited resits. Once passed, workers go to a zone office to have an app installed on their smartphone, and there they are informed that, despite being considered self-employed, they are expected to work on both Friday and Saturday of the same weekend twice a month.

For the newly inducted Deliveroo rider, a shift begins whenever they log into their app and mark themselves as available for work. When I speak to Jamie, a recent graduate, and Noah, a university student, who both work as cyclists for the app in a southern English town, Deliveroo is in the process of testing a feature called Pulse. This tells riders whether demand is low, normal or high, offering them a graph of order demand. Although the feature is in a beta-testing phase, both Jamie and Noah remark on the cynicism and suspicion that the feature has caused among riders about its accuracy.

As soon as the rider has marked themselves as available, the app starts scanning for orders, refreshing every twelve seconds. Included in the app is an embedded map that displays directions to the 'zone centre' – a designated spot where workers can wait for orders. Where they work, Jamie and Noah tell me, the platform's chosen zone centre caused riders to congregate near a local business that asked them to leave; riders have therefore informally created a new meeting point. Even so, most workers do not use the zone centre (especially if they live nearby), and there is a different assembly point for 'peds' (moped riders who work for the platform) because of local traffic rules. Zones can cover either an entire metropolitan area (as in this case) or a section of a city.

Jamie and Noah are members of the Independent Workers' Union of Great Britain (IWGB), a small 'base' (or 'rank-and-file') union with a branch covering couriers in the gig economy. They explain to me that each assignment – or 'drop' – begins when a new order is allocated to a rider via the app. Once the worker accepts it, they must make their way to the restaurant, collect the order, and ride to the customer to deliver it. The app offers a map and directions to both the restaurant and customer drop-off, but riders often prefer to rely on their knowledge of the area. If the worker does not accept, they are issued an 'unassigned' penalty. They can have up to 10 per cent unassigned before they attract the attention of managers. At the time I speak to them, workers in their zone are earning £4 per drop – though that figure varies nationally, as there are different pay models across the country. If there is a problem with a drop, such as the rider getting a puncture or having a crash, the rider calls the managers in the zone office, who will communicate with the restaurant and/or customer and give the rider an unassigned penalty. The app also contains a link to a Freefone number that connects them to the customer in the event they cannot find an address.

In this location there are two zone managers and, Jamie and Noah estimate, between 300 and 600 riders. Workers do not have access to the staff numbers, but they say that there has been a surge in new riders in recent months due to a recent recruitment drive. This has also led other workers to quit, as there is less work to go around.

The two types of riders – cyclists and peds – expect different performance rates. For a cyclist, it's an achievement to reach an average of four drops per hour, while peds can achieve much more. At the time of the interview, ten deliveries per shift is good for cyclists, but for peds the figure is more like fifty or sixty.[15] Some cyclists put this down to the way orders are allocated to riders – a process which is the source of much speculation among workers. In particular, peds tend to reach higher drop rates by picking up a greater number of 'doubles' and 'triples', in which multiple customers' orders will be picked up from the same restaurant at the same time, earning them £8 or £12 from a single collection.

The app monitors where the rider is via GPS, and their location is made available to both the restaurant and the customer. When the drop is complete, the app will usually allocate a new drop within a reasonable distance, so riders will often stay in one area of the zone for most of their shift. Cyclists' shifts tend to last two or three hours, and they can log out of the app when they choose (by using a feature on the app, 'Make this my last order', at busy times). A dip in their drop rate will bring down their hourly average, which is recorded in the app. During peak hours, riders can often take risks in order to earn a higher hourly wage. As Noah tells me, 'The peak period is concentrated . . . So on Friday night, I'd be sitting at the zone centre, and your phone pings, and like, right, this is the start and I have to cycle as many miles as I can before 9:30 p.m., and then the money stops . . . That was the situation on Friday, it just all dried up for cyclists at 9:30, but you know, like I've got, say, two hours to absolutely bust my balls and cycle the most amount of miles for the most amount of money.'

On finishing work, some workers will congregate in the zone centre to compare stats using a feature on the app that records their order history – though most will go straight home. But the process of assessing stats following a shift is a common experience, and not always a positive one, says Jamie: 'There's this constant problem where you'll come in from a shift and probably about 70 to 80 per cent of the time you'll do the calculations and you'll be really disappointed, and that's kind of a horrible moment, because they make it easier, they give you the My Deliveries thing which shows you your deliveries per hour, and if you see an hour with no deliveries in it, you're like, "I literally didn't work for an entire hour. I didn't make anything, I got zero per hour" – and, like, that's just . . . the app literally shows you your earning capacity, and I think it has a great demotivating capacity in a sense.'

The Deliveroo riders I speak to often describe the platform as 'an automated food delivery service without the automation' – an evocative idea that highlights the lack of control that workers experience on the job, and the degree to which they are beholden to the platform's technology. The statistical assessment also speaks to the 'self-employed' character of the work at Deliveroo. But other workplaces take a different approach, with harsher consequences. A key feature of work at the distribution centre where Lorenzo laboured is that each day begins with an automated text message from the employer, which tells workers whether their scheduled work for the day is confirmed or cancelled based on personal productivity stats from their previous shift. As an agency worker with no guarantee of hours, Lorenzo explains there will be no remuneration if he is told not to come in. If the shift is confirmed, he will begin work – unpaid, because it will be prior to logging into the productivity system – in a briefing area at the site, where a shop floor manager will speak to a group of around eighty employees advertising the day's targets and delivering 'feedback' on the previous day's performance figures. Lorenzo describes this as 'essentially a bollocking'.

The IWGB was an early combatant in the fight for workers' rights in the gig economy. At Deliveroo, the union began recruiting riders in 2016, demanding recognition and coordinating 'wildcat' industrial action by exploiting Deliveroo's refusal to recognise its workers as direct employees. Like other unions in the sector, it has also sought to change the law, both through parliamentary inquiries and by advancing legal test cases. Along with other unions, the IWGB has chalked up wins against bike courier firm CitySprint and the taxi platform Uber, where it has also organised drivers. Uber has also been subject to court challenges from one of Britain's largest unions, GMB, a union that has often treated the much smaller IWGB with disdain.

The tension between the two trade unions is a reminder that 'unionisation' can have quite different meanings. The boisterous and often creative protests of base unions like IWGB or United Voices of the World have left the leaders of large, long-established unions unimpressed, especially when their demands have exceeded those of their larger counterparts. GMB itself has flirted with the use of creative tactics in its lengthy campaign for recruitment and recognition at the online clothing retailer Asos, including organising a fashion-themed 'catwalk of shame' media stunt outside a shareholder meeting. Yet in contrast to the IWGB, the GMB's focus on achieving a statutory recognition agreement has led the union to focus primarily on contracted workers over agency workers, a group that makes up around half the workforce. When Asos and the warehouse operator XPO signed a sweetheart deal with the moderate union Community – contravening a convention among TUC member unions by which they agree not to recruit or campaign at workplaces where another union has a recognition agreement with an employer, or is campaigning for one – GMB was forced to back away from the site. Ironically, in 2021 GMB signed its own deal with Uber in Britain, pushing out the IWGB and signing an historic 'partnership' deal with the platform. By all accounts the deal *was* historic: it was the first union agreement Uber had entered into, and probably one of the largest signed by a union without a mechanism for collective bargaining on pay, let alone Uber's algorithmic regime. GMB officials will know that their deal is not perfect and hope to build upon it in time – albeit without the leverage to do so.

It is important to differentiate the political conception of unions as vehicles for working-class organisation from trade unions as we actually find them. Many unions, perhaps most, are not particularly interested in working-class advancement for its own sake, let alone in opposing capitalism. Even within the narrow bounds of mainstream industrial relations, unions have a range of political approaches, some of which are in conflict with each other – and occasionally even with the demands of their members. Practically speaking, in Britain a recognition deal can be used as a way for employers to ward off other, more combative unions, as in the case of Uber and the GMB. In many workplaces, workers have the realistic option of just a single union: many supermarket workers, for example, are forced to join Usdaw, maybe one of the least revolutionary labour organisations conceivable.

Understood sociologically as an expression of the 'class for itself', trade unionism (including independent or base unionism) has historically been concerned with the organisation of the labour force in order to improve the social position of labour against capital. The nature and approach of trade unions throughout history have varied dramatically. As such, it is difficult to sketch the general character of their political activities. But these tend to include negotiating with employers, mounting legal challenges, representing workers in grievances, organising branches within workplaces, calling strike action and engaging with political parties.

Most unions, when they approach a non-unionised workplace, see recognition as the most important first step. In the case of GMB at Asos, initial tactics included placing adverts on Facebook and hiring advertising space on the roundabout opposite the site entrance, as well as gate jobs (leafleting workers at the entrance to the workplace in order to persuade them to join the union), a tactic often used when a trade union lacks a presence inside a workplace. The GMB campaign targeted the company's insecure contracts, as well as improving pay, dignity at work and company transparency. But the centrality of the recognition deal reflected the position that trade unions have long held within the modern industrial landscape. Unions are intermediaries between workers and employers, seeking to negotiate the terms and conditions of work, whose political logic aims toward the shared governance of work. This partnership approach, which supposes the role of unions is to find alignment between workers' interests and those of their employers, represents the curtailment of the historically socialist character of trade unions, and has been a source of lament for Marxists. As the labour scholar Harry Braverman wrote, this is partly due to a lack of appetite for workers' control:

> The unionized working class, intimidated by the scale and complexity of capitalist production, and weakened in its original revolutionary impetus by the gains afforded by the rapid increase of productivity, increasingly lost the will and ambition to wrest control of production from capitalist hands and turned ever more to bargaining over labor's share in the product.[16]

Such a contractual focus does not typically lend itself to questioning the role of technology, except where jobs are immediately threatened, with the possibility of unemployment brought about by automation, for instance, or, increasingly, around the issue of health and safety. Although unions such as GMB have negotiated managerial expectations of pick rates, their approach has been one of collaboration with managers, and in doing so they often invoke the language of fair conditions. Unfortunately, although well-meaning, it's an approach that doesn't always engender progress on the shop floor.

Elaine, a regional organiser, speaks highly of the GMB's role in arranging for ergonomic studies to be conducted at distribution centres belonging to the Walmart-owned supermarket Asda. Asda's distribution arm has an impressive unionisation density – around 83 per cent of the workforce – and GMB has used this strength to negotiate pick rates based on time-and-motion studies. In Elaine's view, this was a means of regulating work: 'They will look at all the different variations,' she says. 'Day working to night working, lone working, lifting, heights, speeds, whether you're a man or a woman, whether you're pregnant.' The studies were commissioned by the employer, but the union sees them as a starting point for negotiation. 'They've got different ways of doing it,' she continues. 'They can click on a button or use a timer on a watch, and then we negotiate and regulate around that, so we know what our members are able to do.' For the union, these time-and-motion studies allow for transparent performance metrics, which are therefore up for negotiation. But the union's support for them is grounded in a unitary vision of the workplace, in which workers and bosses can be united by shared interests. As Elaine puts it, 'We want it to go smoothly, and we want the business to succeed, but not at the [expense of the] health and safety of our members and the workforce. The unions are there as sort of a comparator to try and stop people from exploiting the workers and [making them do] too much, and it's just giving the voice of the workforce.'

For Todd, however, his union Usdaw's negotiations around similar metrics actually made his life harder. When I ask him whether the union is active on the shop floor, his response is stark. 'No, they're shit,' he tells me. 'Yeah, they're really bad.' He speaks about their collaboration with management, describing them as a 'yellow union'. 'The only interaction I know that they've had with my department is that they agreed the maximum weight for these boxes, which is fifteen kilos,' he explains. 'What's fifteen kilos times by eight? That's a lot.'

'120, plus the trolley,' I reply.

'Yeah, that's what you're expected to be able to push around the whole fuckin' store by the end of the shop,' he says, barely masking his exasperated laugh. 'So, yeah, the union hasn't done me any favours, just said I need to have a fuck-off heavy trolley to push around.'

Todd's response illustrates the distance that often exists between union expectations and those of the workers they represent. For Todd, the managerial claims in most pressing need of mitigation involve performance and conduct; for Elaine, the key priority is winning a recognition deal, after which concessions can be sought in a pragmatic way that seeks a balance between the interests of both employers and employees. As we will see, Todd still found the expectations placed upon him demeaning, and acted against them on a daily basis with a range of tactics, even after his union's intervention. A more generous reading of the historical narrowing of trade unions' claims over the productive process would point to the successive waves of restrictions placed on trade union activity in Britain – particularly their ability to take strike action. Despite some fanfare over 2022's 'hot strike summer' – a broad wave of strikes over pay across sectors ranging from railway workers to barristers – unions remain in a weak position. In 2016, for instance, just 322,000 days were lost to strike action – the eighth-lowest annual total since records began in 1891 – around 40 per cent of which were lost to a single dispute.[17] That same year, membership of trade unions, in decline since the early 1970s, reached its lowest point in the post-war period.[18] But we also need to look beyond such figures. Trade union membership and the activities of unions only account for one part of workers' political activity. They cannot be taken as indicative of the whole. Perhaps, then, we need to consider the possibility that trade unions are simply failing to adapt to the new conditions of work. This is a problem, that, in the distribution sector, is exacerbated by their prioritisation of the recruitment of in-house staff over agency workers – a pragmatic calculation on the part of the unions, whose aim is to secure mandatory recognition agreements, but one that neglects to account for the way in which work is now organised.

❧

After its announcement in late 2016, British trade unions began to focus a great deal of their campaigning efforts in the distribution sector towards the Business, Energy and Industrial Strategy Committee's inquiry into the 'future world of work and the rights of workers'. Although the background of the announcement was a series of new and emerging technologies in workplaces, its essential concern was with issues of a contractual nature. It made sense that unions should be invested in the direction of travel for contracts in this new world of work, especially in light of the possibility that workers would see a degradation in their terms of employment. But perhaps just as worrying for unions was the threat posed to unions themselves, which faced a crisis of identity and purpose at a time when they were already largely confined to offering in-work protections.

The conversation around the future of employment contracts in the distribution sector and the related gig economy has been dominated by the broader concern about the rise or return of precarious working conditions across society. The result has been something of a precarity preoccupation: the proliferation of insecure contracts has come to be seen as the key to all future success. But this focus has had profound implications for the ways trade unions organise. Rather than worker-orientated industrial action, unions have increasingly ploughed their resources into initiating or engaging in political lobbying and judicial proceedings. Engagement with the future world of work inquiry was complemented by concurrent court cases brought against Uber and CitySprint by the GMB and IWGB unions. This kind of juridical-legislative focus, often combined with large publicity campaigns, has in recent years been typical of the activity of unions, both large and small. While we should not denigrate attempts to secure changes in parliamentary or case law to workers' benefit – especially given the costs associated with pursuing employers through the courts, and given Britain's strong anti-union laws – their scope demonstrates a narrow focus on the part of trade unions. Given the wide range of problems facing workers in these industries, this is a concern. Recent years have seen unions focus intently on 'fixing' the employment relationship, at the expense of investigating the ongoing technological restructuring of the workplace outlined throughout this book, reflecting an order of priorities well-established within the trade union movement.[19]

While the link between dubious employment arrangements and the technologies governing work is increasingly well-documented, it is striking that there exists a tendency, even in critical accounts, to frame the possibilities for resistance in terms of workers' ability to find leverage in and against the *contractual* dimension of their circumstances. This was true of the recent reports of workers 'fighting back' within Deliveroo and Uber.[20] Although we often see reference to the technologies of management, the response tends to ignore those technologies, fixating instead on the legal environment in which precarity thrives.

Even where there is a nod towards technological managerial practices, a focus on contractual relationships underpins a conception of labour organising that occurs at a predominantly 'macro' level, in which resistance is conceived on terms that are largely extrinsic to the workplace. Instead of beginning at the point of subjection – the work process itself – and understanding struggle from the point of production, unions attempt to gain or force recognition so that they can negotiate with the employer or lobby for parliamentary scrutiny. Given the crucial place that workplace technologies occupy in the managerial control of workers, it is notable that approaches to the issue so far have neglected to consider how struggles *within* the workplace might be affected. While contracts are certainly a part of this, they do not tell the whole story – not least because contracts describe an ideal type of relation that does not necessarily reflect the realities of work.

In a period of significant organisational change across the sector, it seems significant that the primary concern of workers' organisations is with solutions that do not involve workers directly. Instead, they ask workers to join in order to bestow a level of trust upon either organisers or the political lobbying teams of unions, which will then do the bidding on their behalf. Workers must therefore stay in a challenging work environment while they wait for change to occur elsewhere – in a meeting somewhere or in a courtroom. This trend has run alongside, and often conflicted with, shop floor organising within the rank and file, despite workers often having sought greater assistance, and the fact that everyday, unorganised resistance is already taking place at the point of subjection, with or without union involvement. As Adam Barr notes, a challenge to workers agitating in the industry is to assess the everyday tactics workers use to make their jobs easier and articulate them into a campaign. It's hard to imagine a future set of demands for workers that doesn't include [digital management technologies] as [a] fundamental platform on which to fight.[21]

Marketing and propaganda can illustrate political will. The fact that companies spend millions of pounds to tell us about the imminent arrival of drone deliveries or fully robotised warehouses says something about how, for them, human labour leaves much to be desired. Actually existing workplaces, on the other hand, allow us to put workers back at the centre of the politics of work.

The workers I have spoken to may not be representative of all workers, but they do help us elevate the empirical above the purely notional. Many on the left seem to be happier talking about the politics of anti-work in the abstract than the content of work itself, about structural trends in employment and jobs rather than the organisation of work – and what it feels like to have your dignity stolen at work. There are good reasons why the idea of 'good work' might make many of us bristle – but there still remains such a thing as work that is predicated on undermining the dignity and agency of workers. This work is not exactly 'invisible' – these are regular jobs – but we often do not look at it closely enough, and the process by which algorithmic power is being introduced and enacted within such workplaces remains beyond the view of many.

Vague gestures towards the effects of automation that routinely attend this discussion often miss how impotent such assertions really are. Just as the conservative demand for 'jobs' or the 'right to work' elides any notion of the quality of work or the dignity of workers, confining our analysis to the level of 'automation' tells us only part of the story. It may tell us something about the future of employment – but employment is only one aspect of work. I wish to make no attempt to extrapolate macroeconomic principles about employment from specific workplace experiences; but, whereas discussions of automation typically bracket out the content of work, I want to bring it into focus. A growing number on the left wish to see social movements emerge around the logistics sector. My belief is that this cannot be achieved without engaging with logistics work itself – especially if we wish to imagine any sort of movement capable, as Aaron Benanav has put it, of '[bringing] capital to heel'.[22] As the communist inquiry group Kolinko wrote in 'Hotlines', an inquiry into German call centres, 'The way people work in a call centre is neither an accident nor the product of a master plan. Rather, it is a result of the class conflicts over the last decades, and has to do with workers' behaviour.' The point of describing and understanding a work process is to analyse it as the product of a particular balance of power between labour and capital. If this sounds dogmatic, it shouldn't. An analysis based on class *composition* evades the pitfalls to which the formal descriptions of class often elaborated by orthodox Marxism often succumb. Such an analysis, as we will see, seeks to explain the practical relation of workers to the productive process, and therefore the possibility of their exercising power. It is not about classifying workers, in Kolinko's formulation, purely as 'non-possessors' of the means of production.[23]

Critical thinking about workplaces is not a niche academic endeavour. It has real implications for how the politics of work can be approached, in the context of both legislation and industrial negotiation. Unfortunately, however, many of us on the left are a little out of practice with it. Politically and intellectually, we should be dissatisfied with any attempt to define the situation and characteristics of the working class merely as a remainder to capitalist structures. In the next chapter, I will explore a number of management theories whose real-world implementation seeks to undermine the possibility of autonomous working-class organisation altogether. If we claim an interest in working-class organisation and liberation, we must avoid this tendency in our own thinking. For Kolinko, this is a crucial point: 'The possibility of self-organization can only be derived from the fact that workers have a practical relation to each other and to capital: they are working together in the process of production and they are part of the social division of labour.'[24] The other part of that division is management, which is a political project with its own distinctive history.

3

Management

Control is important only because people want it.
– Carter L. Goodrich, *The Frontier of Control*

In 2017 and 2018, Amazon secured a series of patents for the construction of ultrasonic bracelets to be used by employees in its fulfilment centres. The patents' aim, the applications read, was to direct the movement of workers through the physical space of a warehouse by electronically 'nudging' them towards particular shelved items. It would do this by both tracking workers' hand gestures and instructing their movements through vibration, as part of what it called a 'haptic feedback system'.[1]

Although never actually built for use – at least not yet – the idea behind the wristbands is nonetheless a useful prompt for thinking about various aspects of algorithmic management systems, particularly when they are considered alongside the augmented reality goggles mentioned in the previous chapter. It is also useful for thinking about the potential futures of work.

Perhaps unsurprisingly, these cattle prods-cum-manacles were warmly received by others in the logistics industry, despite claims from within the labour movement that the patent amounted to 'Big Brother' management. In response, the website

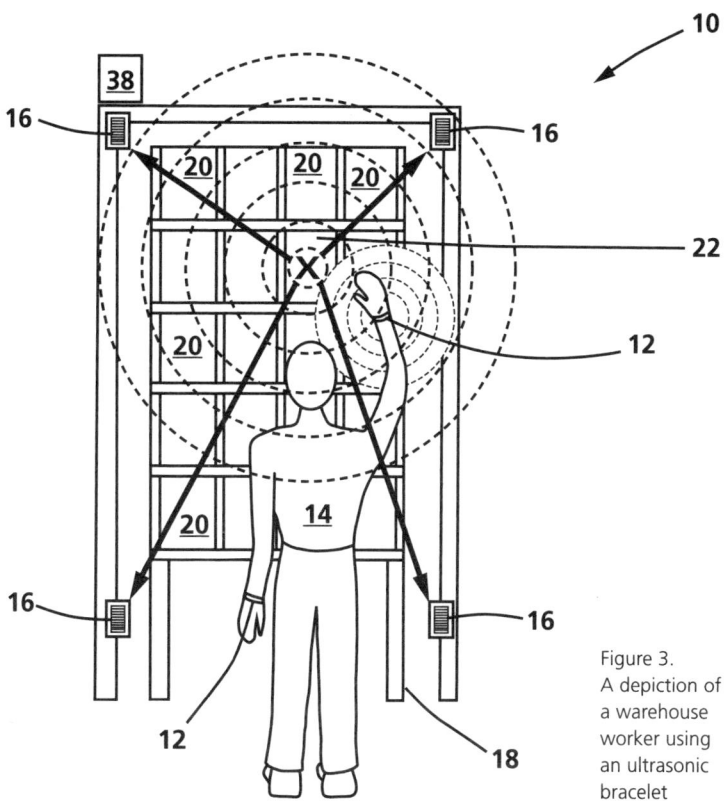

Figure 3.
A depiction of
a warehouse
worker using
an ultrasonic
bracelet

SupplyChainDigest wrote that such suggestions were 'erroneous'. Employee tracking had been a feature of distribution management for a long time, and greater locative tracking was 'likely inevitable'.[2] Yet it remains unclear where the official labour movement stands on this inevitability. While GMB, the first British union to turn its focus to Amazon since Unite gave up its attempts to unionise workers there over a decade ago, reacted negatively to the concept, its accusation of 'Big Brother bosses' showed that, despite the union's formal demands regarding managerial techniques being restricted to concerns about the short- and long-term health and safety implications of the company's approach to productivity management, it was cognisant of the broader relationship between workplace technologies and power relations at work.[3]

Not long after lodging its patents for the bracelets, Amazon responded to concerns about its augmented reality goggles by arguing: 'this patent application has nothing to do with surveilling employees. Technology has empowered and enabled workplaces throughout human history.'[4] Needless to say this wasn't how Marx would have put it.

These designs may seem a far cry from what many would understand by the fairly mundane term 'management' in a work context; but management as a discipline has an intellectual history that continues to underpin its development. After all, it ultimately concerns the organisation of people, as well as resources; at its core, it is intimately bound up with the politics of the workplace.

Management is, in its essence, a political project. It represents a formal and intentional division of power, information, communication and control within a workplace. Different forms of management conceive of this political intervention in different ways. But all seek to achieve the same objectives: the actualisation of labour power; the circumvention of antagonism between workers and bosses (or the achievement of cooperation between them); and – sometimes secondarily – the acquisition of value from labour. As we will see, the politics of management is not straightforwardly reducible to the economic imperatives of capitalism. Indeed, the history of management thinking is rich with political innovations that are largely taken for granted today. Although the managers we meet through life may seldom see their role or relationship to the rest of the workforce in these terms, within a hierarchical workplace these are nonetheless the fundamental reasons for their existence, aside from any other organisational or operational division of labour. Moreover, alongside the wage relation, management at work is the primary means by which most people experience the phenomenon of capitalism in daily life.

Algorithmic management is an innovative mode of workplace politics that combines three key traditions in management thought: the scientific, the humanistic and the cybernetic. Each has its own philosophy of power, information, communication and control, its own influential theorists, and its own political motivations.

Although the organisation of work – even with large bodies of workers governed by an overarching authority – pre-dates capitalist social relations, the development of what we can now think of as management theory and its associated structures is generally credited with a series of innovations that began with industrialist Frederick Winslow Taylor at the turn of the twentieth century.

Taylor was born into a wealthy Quaker-Puritan family in 1856. Having started out as a lathe operator, by the age of thirty-one he had risen quickly to become the chief engineer at the Midvale Steel Works in Pennsylvania.[5] While working there, Taylor became bothered by what he saw as a persistent problem of poor supervision by managers who understood neither the work process nor what ought to constitute a proper days' work.[6] Taylor's view was that managers' relative lack of understanding gave workers too much power over the performance of work – a problem exacerbated by what he saw as the 'interference' of collective bargaining.[7] At this time, the power of workers' practical organisation – either as multi-skilled 'gangs' combining specialist practical knowledge, or in associations determined by craft – arose by virtue of workers' knowledge and skill within their trades. Instead, Taylor wanted to increase managerial power without increasing collective opposition from workers.

Within capitalist social relations, Taylor understood that what is purchased by the capitalist from the worker is labour *power*. Before profit can be realised, though, it needs to be actualised in the process of production. Labour power is a commodity, but one fundamentally unlike all others. Unlike with iron ore, electricity or the raw materials of production, with labour power what the capitalist buys is the *potential for labour*. As Harry Braverman writes,

The worker does not surrender to the capitalist his or her capacity for work. The worker retains it, and the capitalist can take advantage of the bargain only by setting the worker to work. It is of course understood that the useful effects or products of labor belong to the capitalist. But what the worker sells, and what the capitalist buys, is not an agreed amount of labor, but the power to labor over an agreed period of time. This inability to purchase labour, which is an inalienable bodily and mental

66

function, is so fraught with consequences for the entire capitalist mode of production that it must be investigated more closely.[8]

For Taylor, class antagonism was harmful to the realisation of profit, so he set out to create a unitary vision of the workplace in which outputs did not need to be increased through the intimidating presence of shop foremen, and workers would instead cooperate fully by seeing it as being in their interests to do so. To this end, he implemented a new, scientific form of management, completely overhauling the way in which it had been understood previously.[9] At the heart of his plan was the deskilling of manual labour and the radical separation of the conception and execution of work. In this design, managers were newly responsible for applying detailed measurement to each element of work, particularly with regard to the time taken for each task, and training and disciplining workers to ensure work was being carried out precisely. This would be supported by the introduction of productivity targets based on 'time studies', and the reorganisation of pay along the lines of piece work – where workers are paid per item produced – rather than according to time on the job.

Taylor recognised that taking power away from workers and restoring it to owners required the capitalist to become responsible for the labour process and the full activation of labour power. Where management becomes relevant is in the task of gaining workers' cooperation in this process.[10] Taylor's ideal, which he called the 'task idea', was one in which

The work of every workman is fully planned out by the management at least one day in advance, and each man receives in most cases complete written instructions, describing in detail the task which he is to accomplish, as well as the means to be used in doing the work. And the work planned in advance in this way constitutes a task which is to be solved, as explained above, not by the workman alone, but in almost all cases by the joint effort of the workman and the management. This task specifies not only what is to be done but how it is to be done and the exact time allowed for doing it.[11]

'The management' here specifically denotes, within the capitalist work process, the function of actualising labour power. As such, managers are defined by the task of overcoming the 'indeterminacy of labour power'. Management exists to serve the interests of capital, but managers are not necessarily defined by their own sociological category or by their economic relation to production.[12] Indeed, the workers I spoke to made little distinction between the job roles of 'team leader', 'supervisor' and 'manager', viewing their general purpose and interests to be aligned. Early management theorists were similarly uninterested in formal job titles; but, like Taylor, they often responded to real-world political contexts and were explicit about their motivations.

It is said that Frank Bunker Gilbreth's obsession with efficiency extended all the way down to his personal routines. Gilbreth, who along with his wife Lillian, a theorist in her own right, was a frequent correspondent of Taylor, began his working life as a bricklaying apprentice, later rising to become an accomplished building contractor.[13]

Gilbreth first became known within engineering circles for devising a bricklaying system intended to reduce wasted movement, conserve energy, and reduce costs. This led to the development of 'motion studies' (soon to become what we still refer to as 'time-and-motion studies'), a set of novel research methods that Frank and Lillian Gilbreth argued would 'increase the efficiency of the worker'.[14] Such methods involved filming workers using movie cameras, typically with a clock inside the frame of the picture, or attaching small lightbulbs to the hands, feet and heads of workers and photographing them with a long exposure to show the path of the workers' movements. In contrast to Taylor's vision, the Gilbreths' preoccupation was less the intensification of work and more the reduction of wasted energy. Where Taylor focused on measuring activities in terms of the time they took, in order to calculate how much work a person should be able to complete across a shift, the Gilbreths' recordings, made in 'laboratories' they constructed themselves, focused on workers' motions. By observing how different motions could affect productivity, they deduced that there was 'one best way' to execute the work.

The attainment of optimal physical efficiency gained something of a mythological status in the Gilbreths' work as consultants. It was even promoted by Lillian for its alleged health benefits: she exalted its advantages for married life, referring to her marriage to Frank as the 'one best marriage'.[15] Frank likewise argued that unions ought to view the

Gilbreths' proposed system as a step forward for workers.[16] Compared with the stopwatches used in time studies, the Gilbreths' preference for cameras was more methodologically robust, but just as the 'one best way' principle advocates improvement through a consistent adherence to a productive ideal, it also relied on the labour process being stable over time, and on the external and internal environments remaining constant.[17]

Although Amazon has not yet brought its vision for vibrating bracelets to life, the company is experimenting with one initiative that is likewise heavily influenced by motion studies. The idea is for robotic machines to bring goods to workers who stand still at a packing station – eliminating the need for pickers to walk around looking for items and reducing the need for packers to turn, bend or wait for other workers: in other words, to reduce wasted motion. This is an approach being trialled in a minority of warehouses, mainly in the United States. Unlike white elephants such as delivery drones, it is a live system that Amazon is striving to optimise.

To gain a better understanding of the work of packers, I meet José, a Latin American migrant, on a warm spring day on a roof outside a small maisonette on a busy London high street. Last autumn he applied to work for Amazon through an agency as a temporary seasonal worker in one of its distribution centres. On a typical day, he would begin by leaving his possessions in a locker, personal items not being allowed on the distribution centre floor, before walking to the briefing area and logging into work with an electronic pass card. The briefing area contained large screens with a Power-Point presentation showing health and safety information, canteen offers and various workplace rules. At the briefing, which usually lasted around four or five minutes, supervisors would tell the day's workers the group targets, make them aware of any company messages, and occasionally announce novelties like free pizza that would be provided at breaks, or prizes for the most productive workers. José describes a wall with workers' names and photographs, assigning each of them to a packing workstation.

Packers are assigned 'singles' or 'multis', which refer to whether they will be packing one item per package or multiple items, with singles carrying a productivity target of 102 items per hour, and multis expected to achieve 182 items per hour, with results calculated in real time. José then moves to his assigned workstation and scans his pass card, and the workstation's monitor confirms his name, and then asks him to check whether the work-station is clean and stocked with unmade boxes.

During his shift José stands at a screen that instructs him to scan the barcodes of a tote box or a moveable 'wall' containing segmented shelves with a scanner attached to the workstation. José checks items from the wall or tote by scanning them, fol-lowing the screen's instructions. He assembles the correct box and puts the items in, before placing the package on a conveyor belt that runs alongside the workstations. Sometimes the conveyor gets jammed and switches off, in which case José has to pile boxes on the floor beside him until it is moving again, so as to maintain his productivity rate.

Sometimes, however, people take the opportunity to log out and go to the toilet or take a short break, despite the continuous monitoring of their productivity. José then continues scanning and packing, until everything from the wall has been completed. At this point, there is supposed to be a new wall ready, but José says this is not always the case, which will mean more waiting around.

Across his shift, José has two breaks of thirty minutes each. Originally, he says, everyone took breaks at the same time, but the company has begun to stagger them. Breaks mean that José signs out of the workstation and leaves the warehouse floor through metal-detector security gates in order to reach the canteen.

The monitor José uses shows him details of the current item he is handling, as well as the type of box it needs. It doesn't show his productivity, but both the company and the temp agency have supervisors on the warehouse floor who receive real-time updates at their supervisor stations. There are also security stations with large CCTV monitors. If you fall behind, José explains, supervisors will come round with a print-out of workers' productivity scores, and will sometimes suggest more efficient methods of constructing and packing boxes. José once asked how he could check his own productivity, but he was told he could only ask a supervisor for it.

At the start of the season, employees are told that the most productive temp workers can win a permanent contract with the company. José has no such luck. His final day comes when he is tapped on the shoulder, taken off the warehouse floor to a room upstairs, handed a Fanta and a Snickers, and told his assignment has been 'very successful'. And that is that. José is bemused by this overly familiar goodbye, but, like all styles of management, this sort of touchy-feely veneer conceals its own hard politics.

Lillian Moller Gilbreth, as well as pioneering time-and-motion studies, was also an early pioneer of industrial psychology. She argued that, to be successful, scientific management had to indulge the human factors of the labour process. Taylor was not oblivious to this, even if he had less to say about it: in recognising that primary knowledge of the labour process lay with the worker, he touched on how supervisors ought to talk with workers to develop an affable relationship with them, and he remarked that 'there is another type of scientific investigation ... which should receive special attention, namely, the accurate study of the motives which influence men' – though he didn't explore this idea much further.[18] Although it has been argued the Gilbreths' emphasis on combining scientific management with a more 'human' orientation was at least partly driven by business competition with Taylor, Lillian Gilbreth certainly contributed a focus on what is now called a 'team ethos', highlighting the techniques that manage the worker rather than just the work, and anticipating the 'humanistic' management tradition that would soon emerge.[19]

In 1924, the General Electric Company sponsored a series of studies at the Hawthorne plant of the Western Electric Company in the hope of selling more lightbulbs. The popularity of scientific management ideas had by this time led to a wave of experimentation across industries, and the General Electric Company hoped to establish a link between illumination and workers' productivity that they could then market to firms with large business premises.[20] In each study, one group of workers would work under normal lighting conditions, while another group would work in conditions of various degrees and types of illumination. Unfortunately for the company, the lighting seemed to make no difference to workers' output. Yet, to everyone's surprise, productivity increased in all groups, control and variable alike.

The participants themselves attributed their higher performance to the increased pay, the more pleasant working conditions of the test environment, and the simple novelty associated with participating in the study, but the official summary concluded that the test subjects' increased productivity could be attributed to their cohesion as a 'social unit', along with their amity with the study observer, which had developed as a by-product of the research exercises themselves.[21]

The summary was written by an Australian psychotherapist-turned-management consultant, Elton Mayo. His interpretation of the Hawthorne studies led him to found the so-called 'human relations movement' within industrial thought. Mayo's main idea was that workers' primary source of motivation is their sociality. Improvements in productivity could therefore be achieved by harnessing group activity and workers' cooperation. As such, his key contributions were his articulation of the 'social person', which stood in contrast to the selfish *Homo economicus* of most economic theory, and his arguments against what he called the 'rabble hypothesis', according to which managers viewed workers as a horde rather than as an often well-knit group. Indeed, as his biographer Lyndall Urwick writes,

> the problem as Mayo saw it . . . is to restore to the individual the sense of intimate and spontaneous co-operation with the members of the basic unit of organization, the primary working group, with whom he passes his working hours and his feeling that the work of that unit is contributing to some common purpose.[22]

For Mayo, it is at this point that a scientific or Taylorist approach to management runs up against its limitations and, he argues, risks sabotaging management control altogether, unless managers can develop ways to stimulate 'spontaneous cooperation' by establishing an effective relationship between workers and their work.[23]

But Taylor was explicit about his motivation for developing his *Principles*: organised labour agitators. These, he argued, had led workers to believe that their interests were not reconcilable with those of management.[24] For Taylor, there were two key problems in the modern workplace. The first was antagonism in the workplace, which was a threat to capitalists' interests; second, the primary example of workplace friction, for Taylor, was what he called 'soldiering' – the tendency for workers not to work to their full capacity in case it becomes injurious to their own interests. In Taylor's mind, this was a conscious form of non-compliance for which he blamed union organisers. Taylor precisely echoes Marx on this: the problem is that of transforming labour power into actual labour. Creating a workplace with a better alignment of interests – bringing workers' individual interests into line with capitalists' interests – in the first instance means knowing how much work a person *should be expected* to do.

The problem Taylor identified was that factory owners were largely ignorant of the precise productive processes that occurred on their shop floors, giving workers a great amount of control over production.[25] Taylor aimed to wrest control back for managers through the formulation of targets calculated on the basis of managers' empirical inquiries into the workplace. In order to introduce targets which could then become the basis of managerial control, Taylor argued that it was necessary to separate the conception from the execution of labour. 'Conception' refers to the knowledge and planning of the labour process, the development of strategy, and so on, while 'execution' refers to the work being carried out. In separating the two, Taylor advocated a novel division of labour between managers (who deal with conception) and workers (tasked with execution). This is an elemental principle that informs the whole paradigm of management in capitalist (and state-capitalist) economies; indeed, since its introduction by Taylor, it may be considered the defining principle of what we now understand as management itself.

Crucially, the conception stage does not happen independently of workers' execution. The knowledge put into the process by managers is initially gleaned from the workers themselves. As Taylor puts it, 'The managers assume ... the burden of gathering together all of the traditional knowledge which in the past has been possessed by the workmen and then of classifying, tabulating, and reducing this knowledge to rules, laws, and formulae.'[26] To facilitate this mechanism, he advocates the deployment of employment specialists (unfortunately termed 'shop disciplinarians', despite emphasising friendliness to employees as central to their role) who can be tasked with keeping records of employees.[27] As the organisational sociologist Gerard Hanlon has noted, Taylor's case for this type of functional management has at its centre 'subjectivity, knowledge and what we might now call "organisational culture". Before management could manage or leaders could lead, workers' knowledge had to be expropriated and the division of labour made even finer.'[28] By gleaning workers' knowledge of production, managers are able to generate general rules and targets that will govern the work process. Through a combination of targets, piece work and merit pay, solidaristic practices such as soldiering can be undermined through the introduction of incentives for productive workers and disciplinary measures for those who fall behind.

When it was first introduced, scientific management met with opposition from organised labour.[29] But while Frank Gilbreth had attempted to persuade workers of their shared interests with managers by drawing on his own history of union membership, Taylor thought unions destructive and antithetical to his system, which relied on appealing to workers' individual ambitions, even advertising the reduction of strikes as a benefit of his consultancy work.[30] Like Taylor, Mayo also sought to 'close the gap between turning labour-power into actual labour and [solve] the employment contract's indeterminacy in the interests of capital' by enforcing cooperation and the division of labour, and by deploying bureaucratic forms.[31] Mayo was scathing about union organisers, judging them to be socially inept to the point of mental illness.[32] But he argued that too heavy an emphasis on efficiency from an engineering perspective would prevent the full optimisation of the labour process, 'pushing the social needs of individuals into the background and thereby reducing people's capacity for collaboration in work'.[33] Mayo contended that, for all its claims to science, the narrow obsessions of scientific management left the social or human aspect of work to 'dogma and tradition, guess, or quasi-philosophical argument'.[34] He therefore advocated a systematic managerial approach to the social life of the workplace as the key to both bolstering management power and undermining union organisers. In this way, Mayo hoped, it would be possible for 'management to gain greater control of the informal work culture of the organisation through the creation of small-group camaraderie in the workplace and by encouraging workers to communicate their discontent'.[35]

It is not the case that Taylor and Mayo had uniquely ambitious designs on the work process, or especially idiosyncratic preoccupations with the power of organised labour. Their ideas may have laid the groundwork for decades of managerial innovation, but they were based on the simple conviction that capital must have a strategy for achieving 'certainty of result' – in other words, control – over the productive process in order to maintain power over a notoriously 'unplannable' workforce.[36] This is what Hanlon means when he calls contemporary management 'neoliberal class struggle from above', and a response 'to labour, to its knowledge, to its collectivity, to its soldiering and to its refusal'. Central to the control of production today, he argues, is the control of knowledge, and the aim of reconciling workers to their roles so that they present the gift of 'spontaneous cooperation' willingly.[37] The alternative is that, without managerial intervention, the capitalist allows labour power to be wasted by the actions of uncooperative workers.

Collaboration, in this sense, 'appears as the management expertise of the capitalist' – a method for breaking down class solidarity in order that the flow of actual labour runs with certainty and without interruption.[38] Nick Dyer-Witheford identifies this pattern in the introduction of automated technologies to the US auto industry in the 1970s and '80s. 'In North America,' he writes,

union militants understood the new production technique, with its demand for teamwork and participation, as a challenge to class solidarity that blurred the lines between labour and management, and broke down job descriptions and time demarcations, drawing labour into a self-administered exploitation in the name of company identification.

Similarly, he notes that the new production technique entailed a coupling of social methods to the increasingly logistical, 'just-in-time' nature of production in the industry, whereby companies could separate groups of workers from each other across a range of sites by breaking down sections of the labour process, to be coordinated more centrally by senior managers.[39] Management could therefore be understood as a strategy deployed against the tactical actions of workers in their effort to mitigate and manage their own work.

Following the cultural theorist Michel de Certeau, who identifies the key difference between strategy and tactics in strategy's 'calculation ... of power relationships that becomes possible as soon as a subject with will and power ... can be isolated', we can see Taylor and Mayo's early approaches, indeed perhaps even the development of management theory per se, as attempts to generate a strategic *place* for managers.[40] They did this by creating privileged positions in the governance of information and sociality that become the preserve of managers.[41] By observing the tactics of workers to control the work process for their own ends, Taylor and Mayo created a new role for management: a steady hand moving purposefully and rationally, and firmly when necessary.[42]

A frequent correspondent of Frank Gilbreth's at the start of the twentieth century was Yoichi Ueno, who was instrumental in promoting systematic management thinking to Japanese academics and managers. Having founded the Japanese chapter of the Taylor Society, Ueno's 1912 paper 'On Efficiency' drew on the work of both Gilbreth and Taylor, applying their principles to Japanese modes of management thinking. In particular, he lauded Taylor's focus on fostering a workplace culture of 'mutual interest, cooperation and harmony', which he argued were compatible with traditional Japanese values.[43] Ueno's ideas were later taken up by Taiichi Ohno, the man generally credited with being the architect of Toyota's distinctive management approach in the years after the Second World War. Ohno was a pioneer of both just-in-time production and the influential management philosophy *kaizen* – usually translated as 'continuous improvement'.

Kaizen is not just concerned with refinement over time, but rather everyday improvement on the part of everybody, workers and managers alike, which requires both discipline and a commitment to self-reflection. Its focus is on reducing waste and costs through streamlining processes; each time something is improved, steps are taken to improve it further. Within Toyota, the principle of *kaizen* enlisted the participation of both management and workers across the organisation, and attempted to 'redefine' the worker by abolishing fixed times and workloads, and, in the words of Nick Dyer-Witherford, making 'worker suggestions for improving efficiency mandatory'.[44] The idea remains influential, as reflected in Amazon's 'Kaizen programme', which involves events in which groups work through the productive process to identify as many *kaizens* (improvements) as possible.[45]

Conceptually, *kaizen* marked a break with the one-best-way principle: the idea of an unimprovable, perfected system is abandoned. Instead, continuous improvement signals a more holistic view of the workplace and its processes, extending managerial control and creating a specific role for the communication of knowledge within its functioning. As the Japanese management theorist Kaoru Ishikawa argued, managers need to foster a system that can continually adapt. In his critique of the short-lived so-called 'zero defect' movement in the United States (an industrial management approach aimed at the prevention of defects in the quality of production), Ishikawa blamed its failure on the overbearing influence of Taylorist methods, in which, Ishikawa notes, 'Engineers create work standards and specifications. Workers merely follow. The trouble with this approach is that the workers are regarded as machines. Their humanity is ignored.' Ishikawa's solution was the development of the industrial philosophy of 'total quality control'.[46] Incorporating *kaizen* with elements of Mayo's thinking, this approach revolves around what it calls the quality control circle: a regular and encouraged, albeit voluntary, meeting of work teams and managers where participants discuss issues in the workplace, ranging from the technicalities and details of the work process and projects that are currently being worked on, to sources of workplace antagonism, either professional or personal. As an adaptive, continuous system, total quality control retains ideas from scientific management about the reformulation of knowledge to produce targets, but adopts a more holistic, and arguably cybernetic, form: beyond work rates, total quality control is concerned with managing work relations through communication and delivering company-wide control to management through attention to intra- and inter-departmental dynamics. Aside from incremental system improvements, total quality control also aims to defuse antagonism and to promote harmony. As Ishikawa notes, 'A conclusion thus obtained can be understood and accepted by all.'[47]

The philosophy of total quality control is therefore the adaptation of a company's future processes based on past processes and results. Managers, as a company-wide circuitry of control – what Ishikawa calls the 'control circle' (distinct from the smaller-scale quality-control circle) – are supposed to keep track of processes through six key stages: determine goals and targets; determine methods of reaching goals; engage in education and training; implement work; check the effects of implementation; and finally, take appropriate action. The quality-control circle then provides a forum in which managers can engage the 'intimate knowledge of the workplace' of workers on each of these areas. This produces a staged feedback loop that is also reflected in the quality-control circle, which follows a 'story' in order to break down individual aspects of the productive process for workers and to give structure to the forum. The quality-control circle brings to life Taylor's principle that managers must glean workers' knowledge, albeit in a more participatory manner that frames antagonism as an important learning moment that can be constitutive of improvement and therefore the overall harmonisation of work processes.

Fundamentally, the intention is for the quality-control circle to become a mode of sociality for workers. But although it functions as a social space, it provides no respite within the working day. While it may conjure the image of a support circle for workers, its purpose is to solve problems of *control* by means of research into workers' experiences.[48] The control of the quality-control circle does not follow a foreman-led 'I say, you do' command structure, nor is it based on the implementation of key performance indicators characteristic of the scientific approach. Rather, it is a means by which management can control various aspects of the work process by communicating with workers and encouraging their cooperation, fulfilling what both Mayo and Lillian Gilbreth understood to be lacking from the scientific approach, and enabling, as Mayo advocated, 'management to gain greater control of the informal work culture of the organization through the creation of small-group camaraderie in the workplace and by encouraging workers to communicate their discontent'.[49]

Elements of the quality-control circle approach can be seen in the *kaizen* activity of '*gemba* walks', which aim to give managers greater exposure to the job itself. From the Japanese meaning 'the actual place', *gemba* activities see managers walking the shop floor, following a productive process for example, in order to spot 'cracks', identify waste and find ways to simplify processes. Amazon warehouses have instituted both *gemba* walks and *kaizen* events. Each day the site leadership team, including the general manager, walk around the fulfilment centre together to examine its key processes. The aim is to speak to workers to identify any improvements that can be made. Such suggestions can be as simple as polishing a chute to make goods travel down it faster – though doing so may also stop time-consuming jams. Amazon offers a particularly good example of a venue in which these tendencies have come together; it serves to dispel the idea that gathering 'feedback' from workers has any function other than control and continuous improvement for the company.

Situated on a leafy but soulless industrial park between the M1 motorway and the town of Hemel Hempstead is Amazon's LTN2 fulfilment centre. The centre's entrance is marked by a sign proclaiming, 'Welcome to Amazon. Safety Starts Here'. Behind it is an imposing if rather bland tall, blue-grey warehouse building. If it had windows, it could be any industrial park office block in Britain, albeit a very large one. At the far end of the car park is a glassy annex that houses the centre's reception, offices, canteen and locker rooms.

I am here because, as part of the company's community engagement strategy, members of the public can sign up for guided tours of the centre to get a glimpse inside the warehouse. I sign up for it twice: the first time to listen to the tour guide as intended, the second time to largely ignore the tour and look around as best I can.

The entrance to the building is adorned with the company slogan: 'Work hard. Have fun. Make history.' Before the tour, we are greeted by a guide and led upstairs to a conference room, where we're offered coffees. Our greeter tells us that the usual visitors are a mix of Amazon customers, students, elderly people looking for an unusual day out, and people from other companies working in similar areas. She says that Amazon welcomes the latter in particular; the company wants to lead the way for others. Once everyone has arrived, we're asked to sit down in front of a projector to watch a promotional video. It shows us smiling workers and flashy drone deliveries, describing the origins and growth of Amazon, the meaning behind the company slogan, and its various community engagement projects like supplying local schools with Kindles. One clip shows Barack Obama inside an American fulfilment centre, speaking favourably about the jobs that Amazon is creating and its Career Choice Program, which subsidises vocational qualifications to help employees secure jobs after working at Amazon.

After the video, we're led back downstairs, where we are told to leave our phones and other belongings in lockers. We're then led onto the fulfilment centre floor by a chirpy ambassador, escorted by a handful of selected Amazon 'associates' who have achieved permanent employment contracts. Despite the ambassador's attempts to make the warehouse feel both novel and mundane, I can never quite shake the feeling that we're getting a tightly curated North Korea Tourism Board version of the warehouse. As we walk through the site, we are instructed to stay on paths marked on the floor with blue tape; the ubiquitous presence of company propaganda – on posters, TV displays, noticeboards and signs throughout the warehouse – is striking. The impression we get is of stepping into an alternate-reality 'Amazon culture', where the work is hard, but the canteen holds ice cream days and on Shrove Tuesday workers are served pancakes as they arrive for their shift. The guide is especially excited to tell us about the time British country duo The Shires came to perform inside the warehouse as people worked – though whether the workers stood a chance of hearing them is hard to say. On the days I visit, the distribution centre is noisy enough that we need radio headsets to hear our guide talking. Despite the volume, there are few voices to be heard, and it is hard to see people past the storage stacks.

The tour follows the journey of a stock item. We begin in a giant 'pick tower' overlooking the warehouse floor; it is very hot. We're shown how incoming stock items are shelved based on available space, rather than categorised; scanners and bar codes are used to link items with the shelf section on which they have been placed. The primary purpose of storing items at random in this way is to ensure that neither shelvers nor pickers need to walk further than necessary (it is unlikely that customers are going to order more than one radio, for instance, so it makes little sense for a picker to have to walk the length of an aisle full of radios) and to reduce wasted time (it is easier to find and pick a particular radio from a shelf containing assorted goods than from one full of assorted radios). The most in-demand, usually seasonal, products don't even get stowed, but stay on pallets on the floor of the warehouse. Pickers are tasked with picking items from shelves and loading them into totes.

Each picker uses a handheld scanning gun which is attached to the wrist by a looped cord. Scan guns – in the centre I visit, the Motorola MC3000 – are stored in a docking bay, with a screen showing how many guns are docked, in use, in repair or unaccounted for at any given moment. The scan gun has a screen interface which displays the next item to be picked and its location, as well as information about how many items have been picked, and, in our guide's words, 'generally how you're doing'. This is the sum of the information the picker receives. We're not given the chance to look at a scan gun on the tour, but a BBC *Panorama* investigation showed that the gun's 'how you're doing' information is in fact the picker's individual pick rate, along with a timer.[50] Asked what happens if targets are not met, the tour leader says the company tries to find out if the employee needs to 'receive more training' or be moved to another area, because targets are based on rates that have previously been achieved. Anecdotes from José and other Amazon workers suggest that, in fact, either a supervisor will advise a worker on how they can optimise their activity, or else they will receive strikes against their performance record.

When an item is ordered online, information about it is sent via a live database to one of the scan guns distributed across the centre. The scan gun tracks employees' locations within the pick tower, based on the last barcode they scanned. The database then allocates new orders to pickers who are within optimal range of the item, ensuring both that the item is picked as soon as possible and that pickers do not have to travel too far between picks. Once the order is received, pickers walk to the location of the item, scan it and its shelf barcode, and place the item in a tote, held on a trolley. After picking, the handheld scanner then gives the picker instructions for their next order. A picker is unlikely to pick a whole order, but rather gathers items from across multiple orders. Amazon's totes can fit around thirty items each, depending on size. Finally, full totes are placed on a conveyor.

The totes arrive at sorting stations, where a worker called a sorter scans each item, checking its quality, before a screen instructs them where to put it on a trolley. Each trolley is divided into shelves, which are further subdivided into shelf-sections, each shelf-section corresponding to a separate customer order. The sorted trolleys are wheeled a short distance to a parallel set of packing stations, where a packer will again scan each item before a screen tells them which cardboard box to use and a barcode label is printed out. The screen also tells the packer their productivity rate, measured in items per hour.[51] The packer makes the box, packs the item or items, and if necessary adds brown paper for protection. Once it has been filled, the packer enters the box's code onto a tape machine, which dispenses the correct amount of tape for that size of box. Lastly, the barcode is attached and the package placed onto a conveyor, which takes the box to a SLAM ('scan label, apply manifest') machine. In two or three seconds, this weighs the item to ensure it is the correct order, scans the packing barcode, prints a sticker label with the customer's address, and sticks the label on the parcel. Incorrect items are pushed to one side, while correct items are moved on to a final conveyor where red blocks shuttle from side to side. As parcels come down the conveyor, the shuttles push parcels off the conveyor down a chute and into the appropriate loading bay, based on courier. Associates then stack the parcels on pallets (large items around the edge, small in the middle) before wrapping them in film. Finally, the pallets are loaded onto lorries destined for distribution centres, from which they are delivered to customers.

Each day, the management team takes part in a *gemba* walk, stopping at each section of the process – dock, receive, stow, pick, sort, pack and ship. Throughout the day the warehouse is cleaned, but the entire centre stops processing orders for one hour each day to facilitate machine maintenance. The operation also appears to be paused while workers file into the canteen. The announcement of the break is the first point at which workers are seen together; there are around 300 associates on shift at normal off-season times, but they appear to work alone unless they are based in the Goods Out bay, which is the only place I observed associate-level staff talking to each other.

Meanwhile, management are present in a number of ways. Most subtly, there are notices around the centre with health-and-safety advice, instructions or allusions to the company's continuous improvement ethos and television screens on the ground level of the centre displaying a sequence of three slides: a health-and-safety instruction, a short clip of an associate performing a task related to that area of the centre (for example, packing a box in the optimal way), and a message relating to Amazon's fundraising, charity or community achievements. More conspicuously, in the middle of the ground level there is a security area with desks and overhead monitors, and a staff 'help centre'. Supervisors appear to cluster together and wear differently coloured high-vis vests from associates. The hand of management also appears in the canteen, where organised fun or theme days occasionally occur, and employees are encouraged to post their hobbies and interests on one board and their workplace crushes on another.

We can learn a great deal about a workplace by observing it in this way, but we still lack an understanding of the cybernetic principles that operate in a place like Amazon, and the meaning it attaches to 'performance'. After all, unlike Taylor's workshops, Amazon warehouses are not really organised and run by managers as such. What makes modern logistics so effective is that, at crucial points, the system can organise and run itself.

Despite the differences between *kaizen* and Taylor's vision of scientific management, the central Taylorist principle of the separation of conception and execution persists. Indeed, it acts as the foundational organising principle of modern workplace management within capitalist social relations, providing a feedback loop that governs the workforce and determining the standards by which its cooperation is measured. Yet differences remain in how this works in practice, especially in computationally mediated workplaces. As the philosopher Antonio Negri argues, 'control in the literal sense is no longer a necessary condition for production: today control is provided by book-keeping'.[52] But as the sociologist of science Andrew Pickering notes, most information on an organisation is 'useless and can be discarded'.[53] This is especially relevant when thinking about large logistics operations like Amazon. What it means to 'control' Amazon cannot be explained in terms of knowledge, or access to vast amounts of information. The point may sound flippant, but in an era where we have an unprecedented ability to amass data about work and workers, more data can be collected than anyone could reasonably use. Within such an information-rich environment as a modern workplace, it is more appropriate to assess performance and effects than to try to know everything that can be known. 'Information is not about *knowing*', as Dyer-Witheford writes, 'but *doing*'.[54] To understand this way of thinking, we need to know a little about cybernetics.

Cybernetics is a field of enquiry concerned with systems of communication and control, whether mechanical, biological, organisational or computational. Fundamentally, it is the study of feedback loops and the ways in which they make it possible to exert control within a system. If this sounds technical, it's useful to think about the system of forces that keeps you upright: gravity affects the body's sensory nervous system, the vestibular system keeps us balanced in coordination with the visual system, muscles on all sides of the body contract and extend in communication with each other. You do not need to be a scientist to appreciate the various ways in which standing still is a controlled effect of a complicated biomechanical system. Similarly, cybernetics can help us think about how bodies and machines combine with one another to produce control – about the combined biomechanical, cognitive and machinic components interacting when someone drives a car, both making it move forwards and manoeuvring it safely. It is a control system that relies on the reliable flow and feedback of information between components.

It is the ability of cybernetics to think across different types of relations and materialities that makes it important for making sense of 'techno-social' systems that combine both human/social and technical/machinic components, and in particular the ways in which complex systems can be 'steered' across a range of inputs, functions and responses. A key factor that distinguishes the cybernetic approach from other forms of management theory we have explored is what Pickering calls its 'ontology of unknowability' – an aspect of cybernetics that 'tries to address the problematic of getting along performatively with systems that can always surprise us' when particularly complex systems elude representation.[55] This implies a different sense of control from that which is hierarchical, linear and 'flows in just one direction in the form of instructions for action'; instead, 'in line with its ontology of unknowability and becoming, the cybernetic sense of control was one of getting along with, coping with, even taking advantage of and enjoying, a world that one cannot push around in that way'.[56] In relation to the idea of 'black boxes' – processes that *do something*, but whose internal workings are not observed – Pickering details the contrasting impulses of the *scientific* versus the *cybernetic* approach: where the scientific approach seeks 'to understand their inner workings in a representational fashion', the cybernetic approach sees the scientific impulse as 'entailing a *detour*, away from performance and through the space of representation, which has the effect of *veiling* the world of performance from us'. He continues:

> The hallmark of cybernetics was a refusal of the detour through knowledge – or, to put it another way, a conviction that in important instances such a detour would be mistaken, unnecessary, or impossible in principle. The stance of cybernetics was a concern with performance as performance, not as a pale shadow of representation.[57]

Performance here is like the 'satisfactory performance relation' we have when unlocking a door, where we are able to anticipate effects and actualise a desired series of actions without having to know or understand the precise mechanisms involved. What matters is the performance relation between the lock, the key and the keyholder. We can see this ontology of unknowability in cybernetician Stafford Beer's idea of the 'exceedingly complex' system. The world, he says, can be thought of in terms of three types of system: simple, complex and exceedingly complex. While simple and complex systems are, Beer says, 'in principle knowable and predictable, and thus susceptible to the methods of the traditional sciences' – we can, for example, take a lock apart and test for ourselves the precise mechanism of the components – exceedingly complex systems like the economy, the brain, or the company, are probabilistic in nature and have to 'function in and adapt to an endlessly surprising, fluctuating and changing environment' – which is to say they are 'not fully knowable or adequately predictable'.[58] These are systems 'so complex that we can never fully grasp them representationally and that change over time, so that present knowledge is anyway no guarantee of future behavior'.[59] They are also systems, therefore, that present a fundamental problem for management. For Beer, management (as the profession of control) ought to be considered in relation to cybernetics (as the science of control), given that in both cases the aim is to negate the effect of any disturbance to the functioning of a system.[60] For the company, this means developing 'techniques for survival in a changing environment', particularly its ability to 'adapt itself to its economic, commercial, social and political surroundings . . . it must learn from experience'.[61]

Over the course of his career in consulting, Beer observed that companies tended to lack an accurate understanding of their actual internal workings. As Andrew Pickering notes, 'What organizations had . . . was organization charts of hierarchical power relationships running downward from the board of directors through vertical chains of command devoted to production, accounting, marketing, and so on.'[62] But firms did not work in this way. Instead, the charts 'functioned, at most, as devices for apportioning blame when things went wrong'. Beer argued that organisations based on probabilistic systems risked ataxia. If they were not sufficiently capable of adjusting to changing circumstances, such as system disturbances that cannot be determined before they occur, they were prone to dysfunction. Firms must not only continually improve, but must be robust enough to adapt and change course quickly. One proposal in Beer's 1972 book *Brain of the Firm* was what he termed a 'viable systems model'

(VSM) – a way of conceptualising organisations based on the idea of the self-regulation and adaptivity of a system across a variety of components that are in conversation with each other, in which managers are 'positioned within purposefully designed information flows' in such a way that they can steer the firm by balancing interlocutory processes.

For Beer, the VSM presented the possibility of reorganising the firm, for the first time, around the use of computers. The idea was 'to effect a transformation that was social as well as technological, to rearrange the human components as part of an adaptive technosocial system of information flows and transformations'.[63] Managers could exercise control in the resulting system by virtue of their position within communicative flows, where they would occupy a 'servomechanical' role. This means they would be positioned to correct course within the system on the basis of the information being fed back to them, and specifically to 'use feedback processes to cancel out the effects of disturbances on their operations'.[64]

But Stafford Beer was no natural ally of the managerial class. He was, he wrote, 'to the left of Marx'. As a critic of capitalist managerial practices, Beer sought to undo hierarchies of command and control through 'adaptive couplings' between levels of decision-makers to help distribute authority through a system. Indeed, this was the impulse behind his most high-profile commission as a management consultant when, in 1971, he was enlisted by Salvador Allende's socialist government as the architect of the futuristic decision-support system known as Project CyberSyn – a distributed network of telex machines connected to a control room that wouldn't have looked amiss in an episode of *The Jetsons*.[65] Although it was dismantled on the orders of General Pinochet following his 1973 coup, before it could be properly deployed, renewed interest in the project has pointed to CyberSyn's success in circumventing a strike by hauliers opposed to Allende's socialist government. But, as Pickering notes, adaptive couplings that were intended to balance the authority of workers against that of bureaucrats, for example, 'could easily be "switched off" and replaced by asymmetric ones'. As such, the VSM was not necessarily a particularly 'potent bulwark against the institutional arrangements that Beer wanted to obviate'.[66]

An explicitly asymmetric – and more readily deployable – version of a company-wide adaptive management system was Robert Kaplan's 'closed-loop management system' (CLMS). Based on the highly influential 'balanced scorecard' model, which is still widely in use and has informed a range of other management tools, the CLMS aims to extend managerial control beyond a primary focus on the financial bottom line towards a more distributed and systematic architecture of control through the incorporation of company strategy and operations.[67] The closed loop resembles the repeated stages of the total-quality-control model. In six stages, the CLMS threads together the development of strategy by managers, translation of strategy to workers, alignment of the resources of the organisation, planning of operations, monitoring and learning, and testing and adapting. The CLMS is a cybernetic approach to management whereby managers are able to account for, and control, both external and internal disturbances through the effective communication of productive and organisational processes – which is to say, the various labour processes within the company – from workers to managers, which is then channelled into strategic 'alignment' directives.

The CLMS demonstrates what Pickering calls the democratic fragility of the viable systems model.[68] Beer wanted to distribute decision-making within the functioning of the system, relying on adaptive couplings to act as checks and balances across operational and managerial levels. But the extent to which adaptive couplings are integrated into the system – to keep it 'genuinely cybernetic' – appears to be a normative decision based on managerial pre-rogatives. As Pickering concedes, without adequate adaptive couplings, VSMs could become 'rather effective systems of command, control and surveil-lance', used to curb workers' demands rather than incorporate them.[69] The cybernetician Werner Ulrich presses this line of argument in his critique of Project CyberSyn, criticising the model for being 'purposive' rather than 'purposeful' – meaning that, without substantive built-in goals, the system would end up implementing whatever ambitions were brought to it in a top-down fashion.[70] Although adaptive couplings were built into CyberSyn as recip-rocal (rather than one-way) devices, there remained an asymmetrical relationship with regard to goal for-mation, which generally came 'from above'.[71] For this reason, it could be said that, while the adaptive couplings of the VSM mediate performance, the dis-ciplinary aspect of the model (ensuring 'certainty of result') remains top-down in practice.

✍

Both Beer's and Kaplan's methods demand that the system itself is considered a factor of work and management, in addition to human actors. The sociologist Phoebe Moore refers to the contemporary managerial epoch as one of agile management systems – 'agile' being an intentionally slippery term invoking leanness and adaptivity, as well as flexibility and insecurity.[72] As Moore writes, 'The primary difference between scientific management and agility is the even-greater emphasis placed on technology, to the point that we are symbolically asked to "serve" the machine'.[73] This means the precise tracking of the performance of workers – spatially, temporally, and, as with the 'quantified self' style wearables used in some workplaces, even physiologically. With the range of tracking technologies available, managers can track workers second by second, knowing more about their work than ever before, and producing new forms of knowledge through the massive accumulation of data. And yet, despite the vast amount of data produced and the real-time nature of its transmission, no manager can possibly know everything.[74] Instead, an ontology of unknowability persists, complemented by a system in which managers are computationally supported in establishing a 'satisfactory performance relation' with the company through an advanced infrastructure of tracking technologies that connect organisational processes with workers' actions.[75]

A key, though often unspoken, conceit underpinning this arrangement is that the data presented to humans by computers is fundamentally neutral, objective and rational, and therefore valid, accurate, and more insightful than qualitative judgements. As

Klipfolio, one company selling business performance dashboards, puts it, 'Data doesn't lie'.[76] As for Kaoru Ishikawa's total quality control, the goal of which is a conclusion that 'can be understood and accepted by all', data produced like this would seem to put work performance beyond question.[77] Management algorithms take this idea further still: they apply control to data. A characteristic of every workplace surveyed in this book is the presence of some form of performance data tracking, typically enabled by a mobile personal computer. In warehouses, tracking is carried out using a scanner device – either a scanning gun or a wristwatch. Tracking here is typically described in terms of a productivity rate (such as items per hour), but, except for packers, whose work requires them to remain static, there is also a spatial dimension to this labour. Where the work involves gathering items from around a warehouse, the workers' next task is generally assigned on the basis of their last scanned location. In delivery jobs, they are tracked based on their geographical location, measured either by the GPS of workers' mobile phones or a specialist handset. Workers using a company van are often tracked by telematics, CCTV and in-built GPS as well.

This tracking is made apparent to workers in various ways. Amazon pickers have a visible pick rate and countdown timer on their handset displays. Others – like Lorenzo, the distribution picker-packer – receive morning text messages telling them whether yesterday's performance has been enough to award them another shift. Among the people I spoke to, workers typically have to ask for their productivity information, or will receive it verbally from a supervisor – usually if they are deemed to be underperforming. Yet no one could say how productivity targets were set – the withholding of that information being a typical feature of Taylorist work organisation. At Todd's supermarket, targets were increased with the introduction of a new system, which he explained in terms of the incorporation of new product-specific measurements.

For delivery workers, the clearest evidence of tracking comes from their GPS. Lorenzo is penalised for being in the wrong location according to his GPS system, but otherwise his performance is not based on the ability to achieve a high productivity rate. Jamie and Noah, the delivery riders, by contrast, are not penalised for taking alternative routes, but they do receive a weekly email with performance figures, as well as earnings calculations, via an app. Across a range of job roles, target-based performance, whether relating to productivity or delivery speed, is the basis of supervisory discipline, and in one case shift allocation. For Jamie and Noah, the combination of time-based performance and piece work means riders often take risks on the road.

Information transmission takes different forms for different workers. Delivery workers interact with an app or job-specific device that connects to the company via GPS and a mobile data signal. Mobile warehouse workers interact with a hand-held mobile device that transmits data to an in-built radio data terminal. In both cases, workers communicate with what is generally referred to as 'the system' – a computer database (or databases) that manages stock or order progress, tracks the work of employees, time-stamps activity, calculates performance and assigns new tasks where necessary. In all cases, except for the static workstation and Lorenzo's pallet work, new tasks are assigned to the worker based on their most recent tracked location, whether that means the next item to pick, the next food order to collect, the next parcel to deliver or the next route to follow.

There is nothing particularly novel about this, as the history of Taylorism shows. However, three things are striking about the logistical media at the centre of the labour process in these cases. First, the continuous streaming of work data in real time: as long as the device is logged in, everything it does (including 'downtime') is transmitted from the worker to a database. Second, the spatial nature of the data transmitted: information transmission may be instant, but it also matters how and where objects are moved and tasks carried out. And third, the opacity of 'the system': what it does and does not track, how it allocates work, how decisions are made, and what happens with the data. These are the primary elements of what I call 'management interfaces'.

Real-time spatial tracking is to the performance era what the measurement of time and motion was to the command era. It shapes workers' relation to work and to being managed, and it enables the intensification of work. But, unlike time-and-motion studies, real-time spatial tracking exceeds the need for representation. As we will see, this can be both to management's advantage and its disadvantage. The media theorist Ned Rossiter notes that logistics is not simply about speeding processes up.[78] It is also about 'calibrating time' according to various factors and interests. Data gathered about the work process is tied up with these calculations, which entail a necessary alignment of social relations, not over the course of a day or week, or in regular snapshots, but constantly. Everything has to work together all the time, which means process improvement necessitates the continuous measurement of performance.

This is one of two aspects of the management interface: what the cultural theorist Branden Hookway calls 'architecture-as-medium'.[79] Central to the organisation of logistical algorithmic management systems is an ongoing architecture of calibration, which simultaneously involves the location of goods, the transmission of orders, the means of transportation, the management of space, and the actualisation and management of labour power. This architecture of processes aims to calibrate the control of labour in relation to other logistical factors through quantification. In doing so, the 'unplannable' – in other words, human – element of labour is brought under sufficient technical control to allow productive processes and capital accumulation to proceed with little turbulence.[80] 'Turbulence' is an appropriately evocative metaphor: Hookway's animating challenge is to articulate the environment of the aeroplane cockpit, which he describes as 'at once a space of inhabitation, an ergonomics of use, an assemblage of mechanical articulations directed towards control surfaces and the materiality of air flow, and a threshold between human and machine'. For Hookway, therefore, the interface does not describe a technology so much as a way of relating to technology. Within the context of the management of work, the management interface in this respect refers to the way workers relate to management technologies, which – within algorithmic management – requires relatively little involvement from human managers.

Yet this bundle of relations is also embedded within – and obscured by – the surface of the screen, the 'bottleneck' through which workers interact with their personal devices. When a picker carries a scan gun around a fulfilment centre, it is the device that takes up part of the supervisory burden, relaying instructions to workers and performance data back to the system, either to be stored on databases or fed back into algorithms. This is the second aspect of the management interface: the threshold that sits, Janus-like, between the worker and the system. For software theorists Florian Cramer and Matthew Fuller, this threshold is defined by a fundamental asymmetry. It is, they say, 'the point of juncture between different bodies, hardware, software, users, and what they connect to or are part of. Interfaces describe, hide, and condition the asymmetry between the elements conjoined.'[81]

These two perspectives of the interface – as an architecture of processes and as a threshold that masks and mediates asymmetry – suggest different things about how labour is organised within the distribution process. In the first respect, the management interface refers to how labour is calibrated in relation to other logistical processes, and by extension other labour processes across the supply chain. 'Calibration' here can entail timing, pace and movement across the workforce, as well as shift

allocation. As a threshold, the management interface refers to how labour is managed as living
labour, through instruction, tracking, targets and
identification – in short, pertaining to the balance of
social forces. In this sense, the interface refers to
issues of workers' cooperation, which is to say the
actualisation of labour power. Within algorithmic
management, the ubiquity of devices is interesting
because of their dual role, both *in* the interface (a
factor in an ongoing temporal alignment of dis-
parate processes) and *at* the interface (as a threshold
between workers and the system).

As the anthropologists Sally Applin and Michael
Fischer write of the Motorola WT4000 wearable
scanner, the information capture made possible by
the device 'moves the rationale from tracking of
data, to tracking of behavior', because it is used
for both the surveillance of workers' movements
and to monitor their compliance with certain processes.[82] Embodied in these devices, therefore, is a
range of managerial approaches, from the separation of conception and execution advocated by
Taylor and the continuous improvement impulse
of *kaizen*, to the performance-orientated feedback
loops of cybernetic management and the real-time
tracking practices that emerge in 'agile' management. All of them have consequences for workers,
whether because of the generation of data for
disciplinary actions or for monitoring cooperation
with 'the system' or internalising the performance
expectations generated by management, displayed
as a reflection of the worker in the handheld or
wearable device.

Knowing something of the history of management ideas should encourage us to think about how principles such as cooperation, knowledge and performance operate. But algorithmic management also introduces new dimensions to the workplace that force us to rethink what communication and mediation mean at work – the ways in which managers (as the custodians of technology) are aided, and in which workers negotiate their position as media users. If, as the cultural sociologist Scott Lash proposes, 'a society of ubiquitous media means a society in which power is increasingly in the algorithm', then the proliferation of managerial digital media technologies leads to questions about the character of algorithmic power at work and its consequences for class composition.[83] We know workplace technologies are becoming increasingly intimate, and we know the power of digital media can be leveraged against users in other contexts, so it might be reasonable to ask whether managers are now coming for what Franco Berardi calls 'the soul' – the proliferation of digital media such as wearables extending managerial power to every corner of an algorithms' reach, and by extension every cognitive and corporeal action of its diligent user.[84]

Drawing on his research on Deliveroo, the industrial sociologist Jamie Woodcock suggests the idea of an 'algorithmic panopticon', based on philosopher Jeremy Bentham's design for a prison in which prisoners do not know whether or not they are being watched, and its further elaboration by Michel Foucault. As Woodcock puts it, 'The use of automation to manage the labour process creates what can be conceptualised as an algorithmic panopticon. It starts from the sense that "it's the algorithm that's the boss", automatically collecting and comparing data across the entire company.' The result is that, in the absence of a physical supervisor or manager (or 'augmented supervisor'), the algorithmic panopticon provides a means of governing the workplace without physical presence.[85] But Woodcock problematises the idea that the consequence is a lopsided settlement which places the frontier of control squarely in managerial hands. Rather, his insistence on the metaphor of the panopticon relates to Deliveroo's reliance on an 'illusion of managerial control, albeit backed up with evidence of detailed supervision and occasional disciplinary acts'.

Owing to Deliveroo's limited capacity for carrying out disciplinary measures (partly due to its lean model, as well as the 'bogus self-employed relationship'), Woodcock argues that the company relies on close monitoring through a digital control infrastructure (including GPS and user interface interactions) to maintain practical control within the work process despite managers' spatial distance from the workplace. 'The appearance of an omnipresent and automatic method of supervising and disciplining workers', he writes, 'is a cost effective method of control.' This form of organisation inculcates 'the feeling of being constantly tracked or watched' among workers, but belies a 'precarity for the platform itself'. The crucial point is that the appearance of control is *illusory*, founded on a 'precarious assemblage' of managerial techniques within which Deliveroo relies 'on an algorithmic panopticon to manage the indeterminacy of the labour process'. In this sense, Woodcock problematises the suggestion of a fairly incidental lack of transparency in need of fixing, as liberal commentators often prefer to frame things, by identifying a strategy of opacity on the part of the company, albeit with uncertain results.

If management algorithms alone cannot achieve certainty of result, then we might ask: What kind of information will avoid being bundled into performance data? What knowledge will be retained by workers? And what might algorithms conceal from, rather than reveal to, managers? The management theories discussed in this chapter give little impression of the potential for workers to cause interruption to the seamless flow of work after they have been implemented. But we should remember the gaps that remain in the real-world application of managerial models, which, to quote Harry Cleaver, 'it serves little purpose to study ... unless they are recognized as strategies that capital must struggle to impose'.[86] As this chapter suggests, such a struggle involves considerations of ensuring workers' cooperation and communication. Moreover, the increasingly complex systems of algorithmic management raise the question of the persistence of 'unknowability' as a condition of managing a cybernetic environment, despite the increase in tracking capabilities. As de Certeau suggests, the strategic 'expansion of technocratic rationality' may render itself vulnerable to a scene of 'Brownian movements of invisible and innumerable tactics'.[87]

4

Technological Politics

It would be possible to write a whole history of the inventions made since 1830 for the sole purpose of providing capital with weapons against working-class revolt.

– Karl Marx, *Capital*, Vol. 1

It may be tempting to see in management theory the idea that the politics of workplace technologies are simply the result of capitalism. It's a well-established way to think about technology: that the politics of technology are really the politics of the society in which it is deployed. This argument, which invokes what is called a social determination theory of technology, is popular on the left, as it allows us to think about a radically different kind of society without having to interrogate what it would mean to have a radically different relationship with technology. This theory of technology pitches itself, implicitly or explicitly, against technological determinism. Whereas technological determinism upholds the idea that physical artifacts – whether conceived as fixed assets, dead labour or just plain old metal and wires – can somehow hold political properties that make them more or less progressive, a social determination theory of technology sets its sights on the historically specific social relations that led to, or benefit from, its employment. 'It took both time and experience before the workers learnt to distinguish between machinery and its employment by capital', wrote Marx in his discussion of the machine-breaking Luddites, 'and therefore to transfer their attacks from the material instruments of production to the form of society which utilises those instruments.'[1]

The social determination theory of technology is usually associated with Lenin, particularly with his support for Fordist production techniques in the years after the Russian Revolution. The argument went something like this: although Fordist techniques may have undermined workers when implemented under the capitalist social relations of the United States, the same techniques would have a different political character within the context of the early Soviet Union. Needless to say, this did not quite work out as planned. Even so, the same idea today is often modified rather than jettisoned. This usually takes the form of 'repurposing' present technologies towards socialist ends. Even if this position is more cognisant than Lenin's view of Fordism of the need to change aspects of our present orientation to technology, inherent in the idea is the theory that the political effects of technologies are defined by their social intention: change the intention, change the effect. In this formulation, technology remains inert, even if its proponents prefer to frame it as flexible rather than neutral.

The eminent Marxist geographer David Harvey argues similarly. When considering the politics of technology, he argues, it is necessary to capture something of technology's flexibility, while ensuring due weight is given to its capitalist context. For Harvey, this means understanding what he calls the open and dialectical relation between technologies and a number of terrains which are crucial to capitalist development. Reflecting on a key chapter of Marx's *Capital*, he describes the technologies discussed by Marx as being 'suited' to capitalist production.[2] Harvey leaves the meaning he attaches to this ambiguous, only indicating that these are the 'technologies through which capitalism has found its own basis' and therefore 'the technologies *of* a capitalist mode of production' (my emphasis). In his idiosyncratic reading of Marx, Harvey identifies six elements 'revealed' by technology, which form the general framework, he says, of dialectical and historical materialism: the relation to nature, social relations, mental conceptions, the reproduction of social life and the actual process of production. The six elements – technology itself being the sixth –

coevolve and are subject to perpetual renewal and transformation as dynamic moments within the totality. But it is not a Hegelian totality in which each moment tightly internalizes all the others. It is more like an ecological totality, what Lefebvre refers to as an 'ensemble' or Deleuze as an 'assemblage', of moments coevolving in an open, dialectical manner. Uneven development between and among the elements produces contingency in human evolution.[3]

For Harvey, it is crucial to examine technological forms through the prism of this ecological totality. 'Technologies and organizational forms do not descend from the sky,' he argues. 'They get produced out of mental conceptions. They also arise out of our social relations and concretely arise in response to the practical needs of daily life or of labor processes.' Although Harvey acknowledges the space that exists for political engagement to occur across these elements, his analysis generally remains at the structural level. Notably, he asserts that 'no one moment [element] prevails over the others', and even argues against what he calls 'class-struggle determinism'.[4] This is a problematic position for a Marxist analysis that fundamentally understands capital as a class relation, and Harvey appears to conflate the view that one element can prevail over the others (insofar as it can be a dominant condition) with a deterministic position. I would instead argue that remaining mindful of the wealth of contingencies involved in capitalist development does not stop us from maintaining a commitment to the principle that the working class is a unique, recurring and propulsive problem for capitalism.

The political economist Harry Braverman took a position not dissimilar to Harvey's in his book *Labor and Monopoly Capitalism*. He argued that although technology is produced by capitalist social relations, the process by which they produce technology is historical rather than a fixed chemical reaction. 'The concrete and determinate forms of society are indeed "determined" rather than accidental,' he wrote, 'but this is the determinacy of the thread-by-thread weaving of the fabric of history, not the imposition of external formulas.'[5] This is perhaps still the dominant way of understanding technology on the left today, with the place of technology in a future society hanging on our ability to re-weave the threads binding technology to capitalist social relations. Nonetheless, Braverman did bestow upon technology – particularly, in his writing of the 1970s, upon machinery – a special role within the functioning of capitalist social relations, arguing that 'the ideal toward which capitalism strives is the domination of dead labor over living labor': in other words, the process by which automation aims to supplant workers, which is in turn presented as a physical fact of economic development.[6] Braverman saw this fact as being driven by the need for capital to maximise surplus value.

But the economic view of capitalist innovation has less to say about the political use of technology as a means for circumventing class antagonism. It is hardly a novel observation to point out that technology is used against workers for political ends. As Marx himself noted,

> machinery does not just act as a superior competitor to the worker, always on the point of making him superfluous. It is a power inimical to him, and capital proclaims this fact loudly and deliberately, as well as making use of it. It is the most powerful weapon for suppressing strikes, those periodic revolts of the working class against the autocracy of capital.[7]

For the theorist Harry Cleaver, however, Marxist political economy has too often 'analyzed capitalist growth and accumulation independently of working-class initiative'.[8] That is to say, the capitalist use of technology is not merely about the domination of living labour by dead labour, but rather a struggle and a response to working-class power.[9] As Cleaver notes, 'We are presented with elaborately detailed critical interpretations of this self-activating monster in a way that completely ignores the way actual working-class power forces and checks capitalist development.'[10] I agree with Cleaver: what we too often lack is an account of the political dynamics – in other words, class relations – that are immanent to technology. It is important to highlight that this is fundamentally different from saying technology is determined by political dynamics. Whereas the latter position, a social determination theory, ends up depoliticising technology, an attempt to account for the class dynamics immanent to technology is one that seeks to understand technology as an interface.

A necessary corrective to accounts that see technology as politically inert is Langdon Winner's 'theory of technological politics'.[11] Winner, a political theorist of technology, argued for a theory of technological politics that drew attention to how sociotechnical systems gather their own momentum, how modern societies find themselves responding to technological imperatives, and how human ends are commonly adapted to technical means, rather than vice-versa. He argued that theorising technology only at the level of the interplay of social forces was reductive even if it was well intentioned, and that viewing certain technologies as political phenomena in their own right was a necessary complement. For Winner, a technological politics takes technical artifacts seriously by focusing on the relationship between technological objects and society, and observing how the scale, design or organisation of certain technical arrangements can engender technological imperatives that command particular social responses. 'In our times people are often willing to make drastic changes in the way they live to accord with technological innovation at the same time they would resist similar kinds of changes justified on political grounds,' Winner wrote in 1980, long before the invention of smartphones, contactless payments and tracking cookies. It is not that a technological politics should replace a social determination theory with a technological determination theory, but instead that some technological objects can have a dual character which makes them more or less flexible, depending on both social and technological factors.

Another key thinker on the politics of workplace technology was Raniero Panzieri, a founder of *operaismo* in 1950s Italy.[12] For Panzieri, organisational progress is about power rather than rationality – arguments to the contrary making it too easy to depoliticise technology. Panzieri therefore upheld the idea that all relations of production are first and foremost relations of power: capital does not develop because of any self-contained logic, but rather in relation to the ongoing struggle between classes. Panzieri is of particular importance to a political conception of technology because he develops a specific account of the 'revolutions of capitalist technology and workers' organization within the dynamic of class struggle'.[13] Within this account, Panzieri argues that technological progress does not stand apart from class relations, and that there is a responsive element to changes in the use of technology and workers' modes of resistance within the work process.[14]

This helps us extend our conception of capital's use of technology beyond one of a 'self-activating monster' that is either beholden to economic imperatives or whose effects are preordained. Autonomist Marxism has historically sought to understand the changes in work processes and conditions. In essence, autonomism is primarily interested in the ability of the working class to struggle – in other words, its political autonomy from capital. Although, within autonomism, struggle is understood and located in different ways, in various forms and at various scales, its preoccupation is explicitly political, stemming from Marx's idea that the working class is the class that will abolish itself and class society.[15] For autonomists it is therefore necessary to understand the ways in which the working class can struggle against its own exploitation, as well as the conditions within which it struggles. Two crucial factors arise here: the centrality of the working class to an understanding of work, and the need for what autonomists refer to as a class composition analysis. As we will see later in this chapter, the latter is the theoretical and practical insurance against the ossified and dehistoricised romanticisation of the former.

Central to autonomism in all its forms is the principle that the working class is not merely what Cleaver calls 'a spectator to the global waltz of capital's autonomous self-activating development'.[16]

Rather, the working class has political agency regardless of the conditions imposed upon it by either capital, the state, or traditional political vehicles such as trade unions or workers' parties. Although Cleaver is drawing on diverse movements, such as the Johnson-Forest Tendency in the United States and the *operaismo* and *autonomia* tendencies of the Italian New Left, a central point of reference for understanding a specifically *autonomist* Marxism is Mario Tronti's ground-breaking essay, 'Lenin in England', in which Tronti argues:

> We too have worked with a concept that puts capitalist development first, and workers second. This is a mistake. And now we have to turn the problem on its head, reverse the polarity, and start again from the beginning: and the beginning is the class struggle of the working class. At the level of socially developed capital, capitalist development becomes subordinated to working class struggles; it follows behind them, and they set the pace to which the political mechanisms of capital's own reproduction must be tuned.[17]

Commonly referred to as the 'Copernican inversion' or the 'Trontian inversion', this insistence on the primacy of working-class struggle within the development of capitalism is the fundamental basis of autonomism.

For Cleaver, developing Tronti's insight, capital is a fundamentally political relationship; hence political relations should be at the centre of an analysis of capitalism. Cleaver separates the notion of a political analysis from what he refers to as economistic or philosophical Marxist accounts of capitalism, arguing that 'capitalist power over labor is the ability to force people into the labor market, to force people to work for capital in production, and to coerce surplus labor in the labor process'.[18] For Cleaver, economic readings include those of the Bolsheviks as well as those of structuralist Marxists such as Louis Althusser, while philosophical readings include critical theory, in particular that of the Frankfurt School. This raises the issue of the conflict of the labour–capital relationship – in particular, the problem of actualising labour power, as we saw in Chapter 3. But for Cleaver, 'it serves little purpose to study the structures of capitalist domination unless they are recognized as strategies that capital must struggle to impose' against an active working class.[19] Implicit in this position is an understanding of Marx's observation that machinery generally 'operates only by means of associated labour, or labour in common' – which is to say, workplace technology represents an ongoing intervention of sorts into the 'cooperative character of the labour process'.[20] In other words, whereas Braverman tends to understand machinic regimes as largely enacting the will of managers, Cleaver argues that we should understand this process not as a fait accompli, but as the enactment of strategic objectives with varying degrees of success.

At its best, autonomism is a practical and intellectual framework that can give us a more advanced understanding of the conjunction of politics, work and technology. The combined project of autonomism – intellectually and practically – is and always has been orientated towards developing a

new, useful praxis appropriate to the latest technological innovations shaping work and the material
conditions of the present. But, more than that,
autonomist Marxism embodies not just a theoretical perspective but also an actually existing political
tradition with a traceable, definite and traumatic
history. It is against this history that autonomists
have tested their ideas and sharpened their intellectual weapons.

The writings of the early *operaisti* in Italy in the
early 1960s – militant theorists including, among
others, Romano Alquati, Danilo Montaldi, Mario
Tronti, Antonio Negri and Raniero Panzieri – were
generally responding to a dual frustration with the
capitalist reorganisation of factories (particularly
the introduction of Taylorist methods), on one hand,
and the impotence and collaborationism of the
official trade unions, which were dominated by the
Communist and Socialist parties, on the other.[21]
Prompted by the political problem of trade union
officials often being in cahoots with factory managers, *operaisti* developed a theoretical toolkit that
could both challenge the dominant orthodox Marxist accounts of technology and work, and empower
workers directly outside the apparatuses of the
unions and parties by recognising the breadth of
political action and agency within the working class
at the time. As well as being an intellectual movement to reinvigorate the Marxist project, *operaismo*
and its later formation, *autonomia*, were social
movements.[22] In my view, their commonalities are
strong enough to continue to group them together,
as Cleaver does, under the term 'autonomist Marxism', given the open political pluralism and shared

theoretical framework of both tendencies. Crucially, autonomism offers a political framework contending that technology is always subject to ongoing class struggle, as well as a set of well-defined conceptual 'weapons' that may help us develop an account of technology at work.

For autonomists, the purpose of developing a specifically political account is not only to gain a better understanding of the dominative power of capital, but to emphasise people's capacity to contest it: the autonomists seek to furnish workers with the weapons to do so. For Cleaver, for example, the point of returning to Marx and continually re-evaluating Marxist concepts is to develop a simultaneously *political* and *strategic* account in light of the material circumstances of the present, insofar as doing so can put a 'political tool in the hands of workers': political, in that the analysis is able to integrate technology, capitalist strategy and working-class autonomy into an account of class struggle; strategic, in that an account should be developed as if intervening in a war and trying to work out allegiances, as opposed to seeking an ideological assessment or 'critical interpretation'.[23] The autonomist perspective, then, has commitments that reach beyond merely understanding the changing organisation of work – in the sense of the self-organisation of capital. But in order to understand this impetus and the potential for autonomism's application today, it is necessary to grapple with the history and frameworks developed within this heterodox tradition.

One of the major autonomist thinkers, Raniero Panzieri, sought to challenge the dominant view among the socialists and communists of his time that technological development could be separated from class relations. In Panzieri's view, 'machinery was determined by capital, which utilised it to further the subordination of living labour'.[24] Starting from the idea that the organisation of work is, at some level, about the control of the working class, Panzieri formulated an account of the technological evolution of capital as representing a response to working-class struggle, complementing Tronti's idea of capitalist development being driven by the double helix of working-class resistance and capitalist planning. The idea of planning, which is central to his work, refers to the means by which capitalists aim to ensure 'certainty of result' and control over the productive process.[25] The primary unplannable element of capital is the working class itself, which by virtue of its autonomy is never fully captured by capitalist strategy, forcing capitalists also to engage in struggle by continually developing alternative ideas and mechanisms to ensure improved productivity on their terms. This takes the form of conscious decisions in order to ensure that, through the construction of new technologies, capitalists gain the upper hand. As Marx wrote regarding the technological developments of his own lifetime: 'It would be possible to write a whole history of the inventions made since 1830 for the sole purpose of providing capital with weapons against working-class revolt.'[26] But, crucially within the autonomist analysis, the working class struggles back against the capitalist use of technology.

The autonomist understanding of technology as a key site of class struggle stands as an important challenge to the idea that technological development can be explained solely in terms of efficiency. While efficiency is often a target of capitalist industry, particularly in the pursuit of relative surplus, as Winner notes, technological change can also be motivated by the desire to have dominion over others, for which efficiency can sometimes be sacrificed.[27] To demonstrate this, Winner uses the case of the McCormick factory in 1880s Chicago. The McCormick Harvesting Machine Company had long produced mechanical reapers for farms across the American West and Midwest, helping to revolutionise agriculture; but its poor labour conditions had led to agitation among workers. In response, the company introduced hugely expensive pneumatic moulding machines which could be operated by lower-skilled workers. The company was prepared to accept the inferior quality of the product delivered by the machines, undermining the bargaining position of the skilled workers. Although the machines were abandoned three years later, by then their introduction had all but destroyed the power of the skilled workers' union. For autonomists, though, it is important to note that such a success in capitalist planning is never absolute or final. Even though the union was undermined by the moulding machines, the workers were still present and remained a political problem for the production calculation. Whatever organisational arrangements we might observe, they can only hope to mitigate, but never negate, a working class which retains the capacity to act on its own initiative against the desired consequences of capitalist planning. The working class is therefore in an active position rather than a passive one, and has a productive role in the life of technology. Just as technological development has no inherent logic of its own, there is no spontaneous control over innovation. Instead, the labour–capital relationship is perpetually contested. As Nick Dyer-Witheford puts it, 'If machinery is a "weapon" then it can, as Cleaver says, be stolen and captured, "used against us or by us". Or – to use Panzieri's perhaps richer and less instrumental metaphor – if capital "interweaves" technology and power, then this weaving can be undone, and the threads used to make a different pattern.'[28]

The indeterminacy of technology – or at least the recognition that political will does not always translate into its satisfaction when a technology is enacted – leaves open the possibility that workers will contest managerial techniques as implemented through specific technologies. There are two stages here: first, the decision of whether or not to introduce a technology; second, the set of design choices made in its implementation, invoking consideration of the logical and temporal consequences of those choices.[29] Against this, Antonio Negri sets out two forms of working-class contestation: refusal, as in sabotage or non-compliance; and 'invention power'.[30]

This is not to deny the situation in which 'the technological deck has been stacked long in advance to favor certain interests', but rather to indicate the strategic opportunism of the autonomist project.[31] Such a framework aims at an assessment of the potential for the activation of working-class power which sees 'technology as a particular division of working-class power produced through struggle'.[32] A strategic orientation draws a distinction between what Cleaver calls 'an exercise in necromancy in which one or another long-dead spirit is summoned from the grave to direct the battles of the present' and a strategic approach, which he describes as 'something like an exercise in archaeology designed to uncover the nature of the political weapons developed in the history of class conflict with an eye to their possible usefulness today'.[33]

The implementation of machine technology at the McCormick factory had two effects. First, it deskilled a previously skilled workforce. The pneumatic machines did away with many of the skills that had previously been needed, effectively turning workers from craftspeople into machine operators. This also meant the company could employ lower-skilled workers more easily. Second, this in turn destroyed the iron moulders' union by undermining its bargaining position, which was predicated on the skills and knowledge of its members being invaluable to the company. In autonomist terms, there was a shift (*recomposition*) in the *technical composition* of the class and capital, which created a crisis for the incumbent *political composition*. This was a notable political crisis for workers: labour agitation around the McCormick factory had played a crucial role in the campaign for the eight-hour day, and culminated in the Haymarket affair – the mysterious bombing of a peaceful labour rally on 4 May 1886 that killed at least two McCormick employees and led to seven innocent anarchists being sentenced to death – an injustice still commemorated on May Day.

After Haymarket, other factories adopted new technical arrangements within work processes, challenging the modes of political articulation through which the working class could express itself. Craft unions, generally composed of skilled workers and organised by specific trade, were no longer appropriate to a new technical composition characterised by deskilling. This does not mean the political articulations of the working class were stopped dead; in the following years, Chicago became the engine room of a political recomposition: the development of 'industrial unionism'. This was an expression of the need for the working class to organise across skill levels and types – to respond to the technical recomposition of the class with a political recomposition.[34]

'Class composition' is a fundamental concept in auto-nomism. As a body of thought united by a sense of the open-endedness of social relations and class struggle, its value lies in its ability to take into account the changing constitution, behaviours, experiences, courses of action and material conditions of the working class over time. In particular, it allows for – indeed, strives towards – a description of the working class that takes into account changes, both subtle and stark, in the forms and organisation of work, as well as political expressions of what some Marxists understand as the 'class for itself'.[35] Generally, an analysis of class composition will aim to understand two vectors – technical composition and political composition – and the relationship between them. Here, technical composition refers broadly to the organisation of the working class on capital's terrain – especially the workplace as a site of accumulation. Political composition refers to the contours of class antagonism, often understood as shaped or determined by technical composition.[36]

The key intellectual originator of class composition analysis was the Johnson-Forest Tendency, a US-based heterodox Trotskyist grouping that took its name from the pseudonyms of its key members, C. L. R. James and Raya Dunayevskaya. The group's primary concern was the proliferation of Taylorist and Fordist organisational arrangements in the post-war period, which James argued 'heralded a new phase in the class struggle'.[37] They were disturbed by the totalitarian tendencies of Taylorism, yet they argued against seeing capitalism itself as totalising. Instead, they held that what was fundamental was the workers' own power. Their focus on Taylorism had a particular resonance for early *operaisti* in Italy, who were influenced by the work of the Tendency, as demands for increased wages there had resulted in the widespread introduction of productivity targets and the subsequent individualisation of wages – a settlement that was in fact concocted in consultation with the official trade unions.[38] This was a visible attempt by Italian capitalists (and the trade unions) to 'answer' working-class demands in such a way as to undermine them.[39] In particular, Romano Alquati's contributions to *Quaderni Rossi*, the primary publication of early *operaismo*, included observations on the relationship between the introduction of new technologies into the workplace and the changing class composition of the workforce.[40]

Set against the monolithic conceptualisation of class upheld to ever-limited effect by orthodox Marxists, the idea of class composition has been developed to provide an account of the way classes mutate and develop internal complexities over time. Moreover, it enables us to describe both the ruptures and continuities within the working class over the course of various technological revolutions throughout history. In the 1800s, Marx observed the way the machine deskilled and reorganised the workforce, with implications for the gendering of the division of labour:

> Along with the tool, the skill of the worker in handling it passes over to the machine ... This destroys the technical foundation on which the division of labour in manufacture was based. Hence, in place of the hierarchy of specialized workers that characterizes manufacture, there appears, in the automatic factory, a tendency to equalize and reduce to an identical level every work that has to be done by the minders of the machines; in place of the artificially produced distinctions between the specialized workers, it is natural differences of age and sex that predominate.[41]

Today, we are more likely to consider the ways computers and knowledge work reorganise the workforce – something labour theorists have grappled with since the 1970s. By adopting the framework of class composition, we are able to consider the position and constitution of the working class at separate points in time, including its relationship to contemporary technological innovation and workforce organisation, in such a way that we can consider continuities and discontinuities within it. Instead of resorting to dogmatic orthodoxy about 'authentic' working-class experience, the concept of class composition allows us to describe a common referent across time, while also accounting for the historical internal mutations of that referent.

However, there remain competing ideas about the use of class composition and what it means to do class composition analysis. One approach is the *workers inquiry*: a politically motivated methodology that aims both to gather primary findings and to forge those findings into new weapons for working-class struggle.[42] Inspired by the Johnson-Forest Tendency's publication of Paul Romano and Ria Stone's *The American Worker*, an account of work in an American auto factory, later workers inquiries, like those conducted by Romano Alquati at the Fiat and Olivetti factories in Italy, were fundamental to the conceptual development and refinement of *operaismo*, while the inquiries into reproductive and gendered labour conducted by Lotta Femminista were crucial to the development of the concept of the 'social factory' that became central to autonomism from the 1970s.

In his essay 'The Capitalist Use of Machinery', Panzieri writes of his exasperation at the 'objectivist' position being taken by left-wing trade unions in relation to the proliferation of Taylorist organisational methods, which had 'a direct impact on how the working-class struggle is conceived; on the way in which the actual protagonists of this struggle see it'.[43] Although he notes the attention being paid to the technological changes by the unions, he despairs at the way such changes are framed as 'the "new realities" of contemporary capitalism'. In essence, he is arguing for what Cleaver will later term a 'political reading' of the technological development of Italian workplaces. Against the fatalism of the trade unions, whose '"objectivism" accepts capitalist "rationality" at enterprise level and downplays the struggle within structures and development points', Panzieri points to Alquati's workers inquiry at Fiat, published in *Quaderni Rossi*, and argues for the need to excavate the role of 'working-class autonomy in forcing the transformation of capitalist technology and planning'.[44] Panzieri's frustration with the inadequacies of the official political vehicles of the working class – in accounting for both the politics of technological development and the agency of the working class where new technologies are concerned – is representative of the historical motivations of workers inquiries, and indeed the project of autonomism in general, from Alquati's second inquiry at Olivetti, published in another militant journal, *Classe Operaia*, to 2002's 'Hotlines' inquiry into call centres in Germany. The particular methodological character of the workers inquiry has been a matter of ongoing contestation since Alquati's *Sulla Fiat* was first published, particularly in terms of its relationship to the academic tradition of sociology. That said, while there is no 'one way' to pursue a workers inquiry, reflecting the internal pluralism of autonomism, throughout its history as a methodological approach it has been defined by an overarching attempt to create a composite understanding of the practical and political dynamics of workplaces, with an acknowledgement that capital and the working class are specific but relational, and therefore must be examined together.[45]

◈

For Marx, political power was naturalised by capital in technology. As Panzieri writes, 'the worker is brought face to face with the intellectual potentialities of the material processes of production as the property of another and as a power which rules over him'.[46] Indeed, the obfuscation of these processes of control is as much a factor of capitalist strategy as the development of new technical arrangements. This is keenly felt in workplaces that depend on computationally mediated management practices. Although computation is not a new phenomenon, the idea of workplaces being 'data-driven', especially in real time, is more novel. Such workplaces have an exceptional capacity to obfuscate power. Indeed, the intention behind almost anything that is described or marketed as 'data-driven' is for it to be understood as being more accurate and objective than its alternative. In such contexts, the content of data is almost secondary to the semiotic power of data itself: that information produced through quantification and mediated by computation appears impervious to dispute.

Using information technology as a lens through which to understand a range of phenomena – from labour flexibilisation and precariousness to the rise of the service sector and creative industries – a number of autonomist thinkers have considered the ways in which computation and information mediate power through the rubric of 'cognitive capitalism'. This body of thought, often termed post-*operaismo* or post-autonomism, upholds the idea that different analytical tools are required to understand the present than workplaces under Fordism.

Signalling a more theoretical approach to class composition analysis than earlier generations, two concepts are central to the work of the post-*operaisti*: immaterial labour and the socialised worker. Immaterial labour is the essential character of work arising from the technical class composition of post-Fordism. Developed most notably by Maurizio Lazzarato, the term refers to two aspects of labour in particular: labour that produces the ' "informational content" of the commodity ... where the skills involved in direct labor are increasingly skills involving cybernetics and computer control', and 'activity that produces the "cultural content" of the commodity' – pertaining to 'cultural and artistic standards, fashions, tastes, consumer norms [and] public opinion'. Lazzarato combines this with an understanding of work as becoming increasingly intellectual, self-directed, independent and entrepreneurial.[47] The immaterial labour thesis extends from the figure of the *socialised worker*, which, in contrast to the industrial worker, was understood by Antonio Negri to be the new archetypal social subject produced when 'work has become diffused throughout the entire society'.[48] Predicated on the 'very high degree of cooperation' that characterises post-Fordist work, and contrary to Taylorism, the 'socialized worker is now recombining conception and execution within a universal horizon'.[49]

The socialised worker – 'said to be the fruit of the colossal project of restructuring undertaken by capital to resume the process of accumulation' – is therefore defined by its spatial decomposition and its lack of internal homogeneity compared with the figure of the mass worker.[50] Simultaneously attempting to incorporate a sweeping plurality of class positions, from decentralised factory workers to feminised workers engaged in the work of social reproduction, while theorising an unambiguous new basis of class struggle, the theory of the socialised worker, its critics point out, has always struggled to contain its contradictions. However, in the age of the increased digitisation of work, the theory of immaterial labour arguably provides a coagulant for understanding this proposed new class subject. Containing a supposedly emancipatory potential, immaterial labour draws generalised conclusions from very specific circumstances – in particular, the forms of collaboration that seemed to signal fresh hope of human collaboration and liberation around the dawn of what, in the early 2000s, was termed 'the network society'.

If this sounds vague, or even misplaced, that's because it is. The reality for most workers does not entail being highly networked, creative and autonomous. This is not how the network society turned out, if it ever might have. As the political theorist Rodrigo Nunes has written, 'the problem with these abstract points of recomposition is that conceptual development and logical rigour can at best give indications as to where to move. They do not solve, or even pose, problems of organisation'.[51] Nevertheless, these ideas demonstrate that theorising a political economy and social relations that are mediated by information to a degree hitherto unimaginable is both difficult and messy. Moreover, it shows that uncovering the conflictual political interests that have been concealed, circumvented or naturalised within technology requires empirical investigation, with the aim of showing that labour is never completely subordinated to capital. Whatever the ambitions of capitalist planning and the reorganisation of work, it is possible to identify working-class contestation against the impositions of managers. In this way, we can draw out the shape of power relations within an organisation by mapping out points of conflict and antagonism in each direction. The point is not simply to understand them, but to empower workers, and to unconceal the ongoing contingency of class struggle within work, quite aside from any sweeping structural principles or managerial ideals we might identify.

It is important to note that much of the optimism about the sorts of recomposition highly digitised work might entail came about precisely because of hopes around their potential transformation of political organisation. Of course, digital technologies have never been unconnected to questions of political organisation. Even a cursory examination of social movements over the last twenty years suggests that new communication technologies are, if not a determinant, then at least a prominent feature of contemporary political action. Michael Hardt and Antonio Negri, in their unlikely bestseller *Empire*, were optimistic about the direction of digital travel, proclaiming an era in which the multitude – taking the place of the working class – 'immersed in immaterial labour', might engage in 'digital subversion and supersession' through a newly networked global society.[52] But initial optimism about the internet age has now largely subsided, particularly since the 2008 global financial crisis. And while the idea that a network society has displaced an industrial society may fit into Negri's hypothesis of the socialised worker, the issue remains that computer-dependent work does not necessarily entail more mobile or self-determined work. As we have seen, the idea of 'computerised' work is just as easily applied to those who work in warehouses and delivery vans as to digital creatives. Moreover, the idea that the widely observed mediatisation of popular protest indicates any turn towards 'connective action' within workplaces is similarly misplaced.[53] Quite simply, the ubiquitous fluidity of social media is seldom reflected in distribution workplaces, which, while they may occupy a place within a logistical network, are typically characterised by local, proprietary media systems only accessible within the workplace through controlled means, and unable to connect to the internet at large.

We cannot deny ideas like that of the socialised worker a priori. As Negri states, 'All concepts that define the working class must be framed in terms of this *historical transformability of the composition of the class*.'[54] Certainly, viewed within its initial historical moment, the idea of the socialised worker came about because of the apparent dead end of the idea of the mass worker, as well as legitimate pressure to develop a conception of the working class which extended to the labour of reproduction:

> As we used to put it: 'from the mass worker to the social worker'. But it would be more correct to say: from the working class, i.e. that working class massified in direct production in the factory, to social labour-power, representing the potentiality of a new working class, now extended throughout the entire

span of production and reproduction – a conception more adequate to the wider and more searching dimensions of capitalist control over society and social labour as a whole.[55]

But within Negri's analysis there appears to be an overdetermined relationship between a perceived shift in the technical composition in the class (logically or politically inferred, rather than empirically observed in any robust sense) and the projected political composition of this new class subject. Although an initial 'sense of direction' may serve as an appropriate impetus for a re-examination of class composition, post-*operaismo* tends to place a prescriptive weight on a presumed new class composition whose political capacities and opportunities appear lacking upon closer examination. In an historical moment following the deflation of the initial excitement over the revolutionary potential of the internet, in which technologies such as interfaces problematise the way we need to think about control and resistance in the workplace, it is inadequate to be stuck in the frankly outmoded language of 'computerisation', or merely rely on assumptions about the organisational potential of computationally mediated work.[56]

Consider, for example, the disparity between the imagined digital worker working autonomously from a Starbucks and the workers who actually make the coffee. It cannot be said that Starbucks workers are not digital workers – the food-to-go sector has been a huge adopter of dashboard technology and performance tracking. But, as Nunes argues, this doesn't make Starbucks workers any more capable of communicating across different locations than they were before. Even though Starbucks stores are networked, and workers are involved in reproducing those networks, and even if Starbucks workers can now more easily find each other via social networks, this is not a result of the degree to which their work is networked, and is generally independent of the degree to which their work is networked by information systems at the level of company logistics.[57]

Negri's initial frustration with the political insights of *operaismo* stemmed from its seeming lack of ability to keep pace and scale with the development of capitalism. However, a shift of focus from the class composition in particular sites of struggle to the composition of the class at large has meant the post-*operaista* approach to the development of both conceptual tools and political strategies largely takes the form of an immaterial inquiry, jettisoning the methodological strategy of specific inquiries into actually observable workplaces. Instead, post-*operaismo* after the immaterial labour thesis 'derives its farthest conclusion from some very specific labouring figures', presenting 'a conic perspective that starts as an adequate response to how transformations taking place affect what is "close" to it – but then . . . shows objects with more distortion the farther they are'.[58]

This conceptual approach has been contentious within autonomist Marxism since its inception. In the 1970s, Sergio Bologna argued that, with the theory of the *operaio sociale*, Negri had abandoned recent factory struggles in order to retreat into theory.[59] Meanwhile, Comitati Autonomi

Operai (the Roman chapter of Autonomia) pointed to the methodological weakness of Negri's perspective on the new class composition: 'precisely the undeniable political importance of these phenomena demands extreme analytical rigour, great investigative caution, a strongly empirical approach (facts, data, observations and still more observations, data, facts)'.[60] My aim here is not to invalidate the hypotheses of post-*operaismo* so much as to build the political and strategic case for empirical engagement. So far, while autonomist Marxism has enjoyed a resurgence of interest in the 'information age', autonomist analyses have yet to be fully reconnected with the methodological tradition of the workers inquiry which characterised the earlier years of *operaismo*. By following these threads, an analysis of algorithmic management technologies can serve both as a prism through which to understand contemporary class struggle and an under-studied component of regimes of 'control' in contemporary workplaces. As the writer and political activist Ed Emery remarks,

> The new class composition is more or less a mystery to us (and to capital, and to itself) because it is still in the process of formation . . . Before we can make politics, we have to understand that class composition. This requires us to study it. Analyse it. We do this through a process of inquiry. Hence: No Politics Without Inquiry.[61]

5

Algorithmic Management

couldn't find my boss
so I stopped and did nothing
then my boss found me
– 'Haikus About Crap Jobs' (Facebook)

In 2021 *Bloomberg* reported that Uber had hired its most prominent academic critic, someone who had spent years writing about surveillance, discrimination and opaque practices at the company based on testimony from Uber drivers and years of trust-building on online driver forums. 'There are new ways I can use my expertise now, inside the company,' Alex Rosenblat said of her appointment as Uber's head of marketplace policy, fairness and research.[1] This wasn't the first time Uber had tried to woo her; in her landmark book *Uberland*, she had written of an earlier poaching attempt: 'This moment says a lot about what happens to experts: once they know enough to be a threat, the companies they study will try to absorb them.'[2]

Rosenblat's aim – to 'get the company to take into consideration the experiences and point of view of drivers' – reflects the agenda of liberal academics in the field: to put humans at the centre of the algorithm. Similarly, an influential 2015 study by a group of data scientists that included interviews with both drivers for Uber and Lyft and their passengers, as well as archival analysis of driver forums and company communications, identified a number of flaws in the relationship between algorithmic management and human workers. The answer, they argued, was for existing algorithmic management practices to afford greater consideration to the workers who used the platforms. What algorithmically managed workplaces needed to do was to 'support human workers to work with intelligent machines not only in an effective, but also a satisfying and meaningful way'.[3] The study identified a problem of cooperation from drivers, which it said was caused by the lack of transparency drivers experience in relation to the assignments they are offered. It explained that drivers receive an assignment offer with limited geographical information, no rationale, and a short time frame within which to decide to accept or reject it; there were also concerns with the practice of surge pricing. The shortcoming of the 'supply-demand control algorithms', it found, was that they 'were originally designed to solve mathematical optimization problems that involve non-human entities', rather than human behaviour.[4]

So far, so descriptive. But the solution offered by such liberal critiques of algorithmic management centres on workers' cooperation with management and the building of greater trust in managerial decisions. What is needed, they say, is 'algorithmic transparency' – a demand now being taken up by trade unions, which in practice amounts to little more than explaining the reasons behind algorithmic decisions to workers, rather than giving them direct input into those decisions.

The reason for raising the ideal of 'transparency' has less to do with flattening the power asymmetries of the workplace than with ensuring better adherence to the algorithmic system. Mistrust in the system leads to workers using their own sense; it is better for companies if workers bracket their own judgement in favour of the instructions they are issued. In following their own initiative, drivers cease to cooperate with (in the case of Uber and Lyft) the app – and therefore with the algorithm and the company – in the intended way, which subverts the aims of the process as it has been constructed by the platform. In the absence of transparency and a rationale for the information given to them, drivers are inadvertently liable to act in ways the system finds suboptimal.

It's not that liberal critics of algorithmic work don't think transparency would improve equality within workplaces. The question is what they mean by this. In the study mentioned above, the researchers acknowledged that companies might be 'unwilling or unable to share the underlying mechanisms of their assignment algorithms' because they might be proprietary technologies, or because a 'degree of user ignorance' might be desirable to 'prevent the system from being gamed' by workers. In other words, it's not that liberal critics fail to understand that workers and managers have different interests: it's that they don't think workers really ought to have more control than companies. As they write in a subsequent report, the challenge is: 'How do we promote transparency to earn workers' trust but also prevent workers from gaming the system?'

Against this, what the question of transparency should do is heighten the need for a political analysis which is able to transcend the impulse to find a technical solution to the problems workers face in algorithmically managed work environments. A political analysis encourages us to think about the ways in which humans are already centred within algorithmic management – namely, as workers – such as the way 'user ignorance' can be desired by companies, and therefore intended or planned. Seeing the workplace as a site of contestation between conflicting interests gives us a route into these questions. It allows us to see the tension between algorithmic instructions and workers' compliance as more than just a misunderstanding or design flaw. It also forces us to ask if workers are in fact ignorant of the rationale behind decisions, or whether they are acting intentionally.

Without a political analysis, it is possible to be lured into a sort of algorithmic tunnel vision, whereby a desire to see improvements in the algorithmically managed workplace leads to a presumption that appropriate algorithmic adjustments will produce a friction-free workplace. We should ask ourselves: Is our goal really to find the degree of transparency that would be permissible to managers of companies before igniting fears about workers taking too much control? What is missing is a question about whether the current degree of opacity – the withholding of information – is in fact a considered approach on the part of the company. Moreover, current acts of worker noncompliance are assumed to be due to a breakdown in communication between the algorithm and the worker. If it is in fact the case that worker noncompliance is a result of something like *refusal*, then the problems raised by the liberal critique may not be solved by greater transparency anyway. We can imagine a scenario in which Uber or Lyft made their processes more transparent, and yet workers decided to make the same decisions as they do now, unswayed by overtures to 'group optimisation'.[5]

In such a case, we can imagine the need that would arise for stronger managerial intervention, in order to ensure that workers act as they are intended to within the newly human-centred managerial system. In any case, we can see the need to understand the relationships between algorithms, workers and managers in terms not only of 'interaction', but of how algorithms work as a 'social software' by existing 'as part of assemblages that include hardware, data structures (such as lists, databases, memory, etc.), and the behaviours and actions of bodies'.[6] To ground this perspective, we can consider, for example, Trebor Scholz's comment that 'currently, digital labor appears to be the shiny, sharp tip of a gargantuan spear of neoliberalism made up of deregulation, inequality, union busting, and a shift from employment to low-wage temporary contracts'.[7]

So, algorithmic management is about more than just the rational organisation of processes. And, although the term algorithmic management might induce us to focus on the specificities of particular algorithms, an explanation of specific algorithms as technical artifacts would not necessarily assist a critical analysis of algorithmically mediated work as a sociopolitical imaginary. Even if barriers of access could be overcome and sections of code could be obtained, it is not clear that we would find in them the hidden principles of algorithmic management.

As the cultural anthropologist Nick Seaver argues, 'press on any algorithmic decision and you will find many human ones'.[8] Instead, we need to consider algorithmic management as a political framework built on the principles laid out in the previous chapter – performance, improvement, unknowability and so on – with the aim of arriving at an account of the algorithmic management system on its own terms.

A little after his season inside an Amazon warehouse, José began driving for Amazon Flex, a delivery platform connecting him to fulfilment centres via a smartphone app. The app advertises time slots when he can take his car to the warehouse and pick up parcels for delivery, usually either the same day or the next. Drivers are generally expected to take as many parcels as will fit in their car, José tells me, a normal amount being around forty. After this, he uses the app in conjunction with his smartphone to track the delivery route using GPS, and to record the delivery of parcels using its camera as a scanner. José is paid for a four-hour slot, during which time he can usually deliver between thirty-five to forty-five parcels. If he has not completed all the deliveries in that time, he has little option but to continue; if he logs out without having delivered all the parcels, the app may not pay him. On the other hand, if José finishes all his deliveries early, he still gets paid for the full four hours.

Flex is something like the app-based version of the SMS-based shift-allocation systems used by distribution centre workers such as Lorenzo in London. Both communicate with workers remotely, informing them whether their labour is needed and at what time. However, the Flex tool is not based on productivity, and therefore is not a disciplinary tool, unlike Lorenzo's text messages. Rather than commanding or denying attendance, Flex advertises a choice of shifts to its formally self-employed workers as demand is generated. 'I have to check the [job] offers every day,' José tells me. 'I can [even check] the offers the same day. Sometimes you have blocks in a short time that you can [get at] short notice, but you take the risk – it's not every day like this. Sometimes you can go in the morning, "Oh, I want to go today at 11 o'clock" and at 8 o'clock you check and maybe there's not any block until 5 . . . Okay, I accept it or I take the risk tomorrow, but maybe next day there's still no blocks until 4 o'clock.' But the effect is still a binary that ensures the exact supply of labour needed to fulfil the tasks required is in place. Workers are either wanted or not, explicitly; accepting a collection slot in the app means accepting the work.

Another system, Pulse, is a tool built into Jamie and Noah's Deliveroo app. It tells riders whether demand is high, medium or low, and approaches labour allocation in a different way. As far as Jamie and Noah are concerned, what Pulse says about demand appears to have a weak correlation to the actual demand for riders. This could be because the function is, at the time of our interview, still in the beta-testing phase. But Jamie suspects that it is a design feature intended to dupe workers into logging onto the app, potentially at the expense of their earnings if demand turns out to be low. 'I wouldn't trust it as far as I could throw it,' he says. This approach is continuous, rather than binary. There is only ever high, medium or low demand, never no demand, and these levels appear to correlate to busy, normal or less busy times, respectively, rather than bearing any relation to the number of riders logged in and available.[9] Whereas Flex workers are kept at a distance from the work process – their ability to access it at all is tightly regulated through bounded 'offers' or time slots – Pulse aims to ensure the over-supply of labour rather than a matching of supply with demand, so that there are always riders available whenever a delivery comes through. As Noah tells me,

> You have to remember that it doesn't bother them whether you turn up to work and earn much money, so I take quite a cynical view of those, like, demand management tools because in their ideal world all their workers are working all the time and they're paying them nothing because it costs them nothing to have a rider sitting there doing shit all.

This is made possible because riders are paid per delivery rather than for the time they are logged in. As such, Pulse 'entices' rather than advertises; the actual work allocation is done by the algorithm after riders have logged in, and even in periods of 'high demand' there is no guarantee of work.

Flex and Pulse offer contrasting approaches to worker engagement, processing in different ways the formal choice that exists around work assignment in the gig economy. Both tools are used by their respective platforms to ensure there is a labour supply in place to meet the demand for distribution;

neither company technically employs its delivery workers, so while the apps' users form the labour pool in a sense, the Flex and Pulse tools are mechanisms for ensuring that each company only pays for the labour time it wants to purchase. To do this, both apps rely on contacting workers 'out-of-hours', in that Flex and Pulse are both constantly available to workers without their having to log in or accept an assignment, and they both assume that off-duty workers will use the tools to decide whether to take on future work assignments (the immediate future, in the case of Pulse, the near-future in the case of Flex).

Scrutiny of such precarious forms of work tends to focus on the terms of employment, variously described as casual, precarious or bogus, but Flex and Pulse show us how casual contracts are made workable for the companies by facilitating the activation of dormant workers. In the case of Flex, we can see how technology allows the labour process to be based on casual work. Labour is no less crucial to the work process, but it can now be organised in such a way that workers are kept away from sections of it until they are required. Because e-commerce delivery drivers, in particular, enter the work process at a later stage of distribution, the company can assess how many deliveries need to be made, and therefore precisely how many drivers are required – although distribution centres that employ workers (whether directly or through an agency) are able to use contractual stipulations to achieve a similar effect.

Riders for food-delivery platforms also enter the labour process at a late stage. But Deliveroo approaches this issue differently. Although formally similar to Amazon, the delivery of hot food demands a more immediate allocation of labour – clearly, a Flex-style system of advertised delivery slots would not be fit for purpose. Deliveroo's business model therefore necessitates an available pool of ready workers, which allows the company to advertise estimated delivery times to customers. In contrast with Flex, where slots are advertised to all drivers who have the app, the food-delivery platform measures its pool of available workers by requiring riders to log into the app – a threshold that, once crossed, means that riders can be allocated jobs and penalised for refusing to accept orders; in other words, the threshold beyond which workers are on company time and must make themselves available. Riders are not remunerated for the time they spend waiting while logged in, though they are penalised for turning work down. The role of Pulse is to encourage riders to cross that threshold by setting an expectation (unreliably, according to Jamie and Noah) of how much time they can expect to spend idle – therefore unpaid – once they are in. As with Flex, this is a 'lean' approach to work allocation that benefits the company by reducing the unproductive labour time it pays for, but Pulse represents a novel way to encourage workers to cross the factory gate unpaid with the uncertain promise of work on the other side.[10]

After algorithmic workers of all kinds have entered the workplace, work begins once they have logged on to a computational device, most commonly a handheld scanner.[11] At this point, the workflow begins – understood here not as the flow of goods and processes across the whole productive process, but as the rhythmic performance of tasks that constitute the actual process of working. Put simply, this is the point at which the worker has settled into their shift and begins to get on with the job at hand. For every worker I spoke to, there would come a point, after

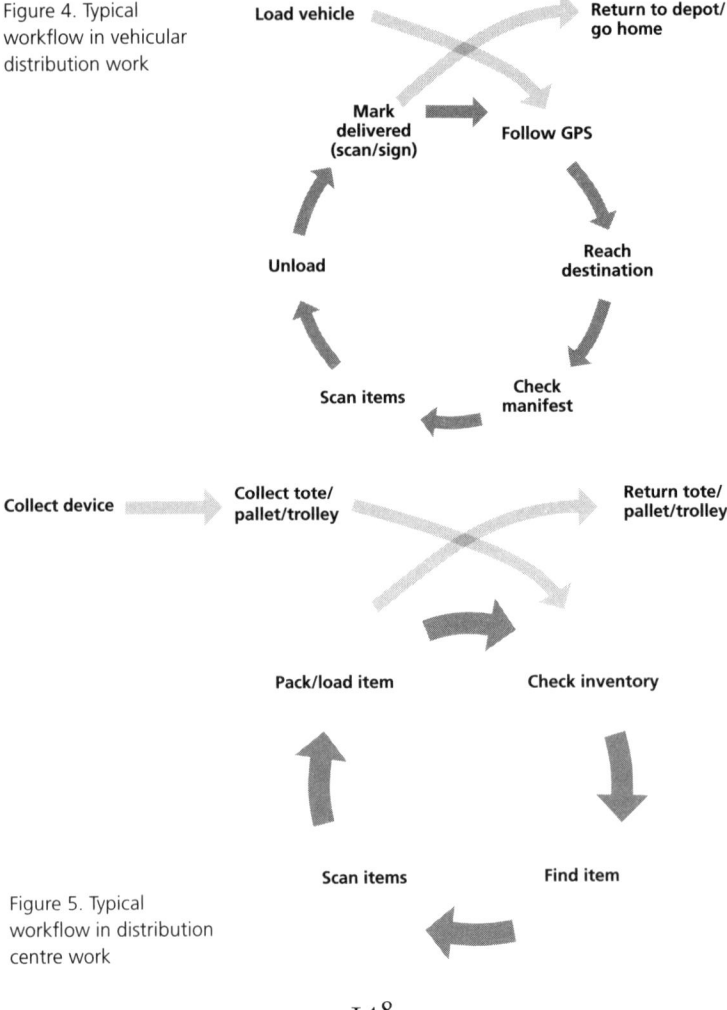

Figure 4. Typical workflow in vehicular distribution work

Load vehicle

Return to depot/ go home

Mark delivered (scan/sign)

Follow GPS

Reach destination

Unload

Scan items

Check manifest

Collect device

Collect tote/ pallet/trolley

Return tote/ pallet/trolley

Pack/load item

Check inventory

Scan items

Find item

Figure 5. Typical workflow in distribution centre work

they described how the workday starts, beyond which 'then you just go on like that . . .': receiving instructions, finding items, scanning, loading – and repeating. These periods, which constitute the bulk of the working day, are when the worker and their handheld device work together most intimately. For managers, this is the key period of data-gathering and productive labour time. For workers, it is the time in which their experience of the work process is most consistently shaped. Vehicular distribution work and warehouse-type distribution work have different but comparable workflows.[12] As shown in Figures 4 and 5, there are entry and exit points which can either mark the end of a shift or the end of a 'shop', but the central repeated workflow (in the darker shade) is largely consistent through the shift.[13]

The fundamental basis of this type of work, in one way or another, is the following of instructions set by a personal computational device. But the degree to which this softwarisation has brought about a standardisation of labour is ambiguous. As the media theorist Franco 'Bifo' Berardi has written,

> We can say that the digitalization of the labor process has made any labor the same from an ergonomic and physical point of view since we all do the same thing: we sit in front of a screen and we type on a keyboard. Our activity is later transformed by a concatenation of machines into . . . the moving of forty metal boxes or a restaurant's provisioning.[14]

Yet, he continues, we also know that at the same time the content of what we do can be completely different, so we could also say the work has become more specialised – although it wouldn't take long to gain an operational knowledge of another job, due to the simplification of labour involved. As we now know, the devices involved in the work discussed here require more than simply sitting 'in front of a screen'; yet the presence of the screen, and indeed being present to the screen, are fundamental elements of the workflow in each case, regardless of whatever else workers are expected to do. Much of the skill involved in successfully carrying out the work, then, boils down to successfully acting on the basis of a digital interface – much like the skill of driving safely is as much about acting on the prompts on a dashboard as the ability to coordinate oneself and take account of one's surroundings.[15]

The organisation of workflow facilitated by the personal data terminal also affects the way work is structured and experienced. An algorithmic management system is able to direct workers and control their manifests (in other words, their task duties) in real time, reducing the technical need for group-oriented plans of action directed by human managers, or even the need for workers all to begin their shifts at the same time. Events such as team briefings serve more humanistic or ideological purposes here, reminding workers of their targets, or even of the company's purported values, rather than being a technical requirement to orientate workers to the day's tasks.[16] They are a social and political choice; hence, they are present in some places and not in others.

Changes in the management system at the Sainsbury's online shopping department, for example, have meant a reduction in shared start locations, with a knock-on effect for the sociality of the work:

> With the new system there is no dedicated starting point for each shop. Now shops can start half way through Ambient 1 and go on Ambient 2, and vice versa. The biggest concern here is that it will be harder to tell who is on each shop with you. Before I'd be able to ask a mate if they were on Ambient 2 next, and if we both were then we'd be able to go around chatting. Now we can't rely on that.[17]

While attempts to stop workers talking are not novel to algorithmic management, there is a breakdown of sociality that is a by-product of the organisation of workflow for an algorithmically managed worker. As the anthropologist Natasha Dow Schüll writes in her study of Las Vegas gambling machines, these techniques of behavioural management in industrial and disciplinary environments share much in common with the 'profit logic of temporal discipline' in gambling machine design. Most strikingly, Schüll focuses on how the ambition of 'continuous gaming productivity' is delivered by the promotion of an 'embodied relation' between gambler and machine. Machine gamblers enter a state of 'flow' in which they lose their sense of time, and, according to casino design guru Bill Friedman, 'their sense of reality, existing only for the moment, for the next bet' as their 'embodied experience in the material world is exchanged for a timeless flow of repeating moments'.[18]

Schüll's account is useful for thinking about how control is iterated in the relationship between user and device. In particular, she highlights how psychologist Mihaly Csikszentmihalyi's original use of the term 'flow' becomes subjugated to economic logic. Csikszentmihalyi intended to illustrate the state of absorption in which one's attention is so concentrated that time, troubles and even the wider world seem to fade away. Schüll details the way this is reinforced and harvested by 'the configuration of the machine, whose programmatic interactive parameters allow gamblers little in the way of tactical or performative improvisation'.[19] This is politically salient when thinking about the embodied, rhythmic relation between workers and personal devices. As Ned Rossiter notes, 'The possession of time by any kind of worker is the condition of possibility for the organization of labour.'[20] We can think of this in terms not only of individual access to time, but of collective access to 'shared time' across the workforce. The BBC *Panorama* documentary, 'Amazon: The Truth Behind the Click', gives a sense of the urgency felt by Amazon workers as they race against their devices to achieve their targets.[21] Yet it is a strange sense of time that the device produces, in which the worker's ability to control their own time is repeatedly reduced to the next twelve seconds in which they must find and pick their next item. Like the goods in the warehouse, workers are forever just-in-time, a lean, flowing force whose actions play out for twelve seconds at a time before being reset.[22] As Rossiter argues, 'Logistics robs living labor of time. At the level of labor management, logistics registers the calculation of time against the performance of tasks and movement of things.'[23] If algorithmic management devices contribute to the production of a continuous present, then, as well as the denial of the worker's foresight into the future, we should also consider the relegation of the need for memory. The worker has no need to learn from past experience, to be able to recall working patterns or routes, or to be able to recall details of the day in order to colour in productivity print-outs; instead, memory is outsourced to the algorithmic management system in abstracted, quantifiable terms.

At the most fundamental level, these electronic devices enable rapid communication between, on the one hand, workers, and their labour at the point of its performance, and, on the other, the managerial system, distributed across a number of databases. Aside from such data communication, algorithmic management also has a powerful and deleterious effect on human communication.

The handheld scanners used by workers act as a site of instruction, command, inventory, recording, tracking, seeing, and transmission – and therefore communication and control – within the work environment, operating as a logistical interface that connects orders to workers in real time. But they also act as a 'point of juncture' between workers and management: workers interact with the device via its display, scanner and positioning system throughout the course of their workflow, which updates databases on the progress of a given job or set of tasks in real time.[24] Meanwhile, the management system provides workers with tasks or instructions, and sometimes targets, and provides shop floor managers and supervisors with information about workers' productivity. As such, the device is the threshold between the realm of work's execution, to be carried out by the worker, and work's conception – the employer's business beyond the worker's reach.[25] By calculating the relationship between time and actions (as well as space, as we will see), the algorithmic management system provides managers with choices about how to scrutinise workers' performance against targets – in the group setting of the briefing, for instance, or one-on-one on the shopfloor, via text message or by making workers compete against each other like the television monitors in Lorenzo's supermarket distribution centre.

Disciplinary measures are generally the culmination of a process of data mediation beginning with the use of the handheld device. This leads to anxiety about the degree to which devices track and transmit an accurate reflection of the work carried out, and in particular whether the metrics against which workers' performance is scrutinised are able to account for mitigating circumstances. In general, such contextual and contingent factors as items being in the wrong place, or the inventory being inaccurate, are not accounted for within the productivity system, which usually appears to be calculated simply as completed actions divided by logged time (for example, items processed per hour). One exception is Lorenzo's distribution centre, where, upon making a mistake, workers have to find a supervisor who can use a special code to log the handset out of the productivity system, giving the supervisor time to rectify the issue. The time spent locating a supervisor, however, negatively affects the workers' productivity score, which in Lorenzo's case is directly linked to shift allocation. It is important to note that workers' productivity scores are a predominantly political device intended to ensure the maximum actualisation of labour power. For all the workers I spoke to, reaching 100 per cent of their target is a rare occurrence. In Lorenzo's supermarket distribution centre, successful shift allocation depends on achieving around 90 to 95 per cent of the defined target. During José's time at Amazon, it appears that the targets were more or less unachievable. José says, 'I talked to all the people, and I talked to permanent staff that had been there for a year, nine months, seven months. I said to them, "Right, I just talked to our colleagues and they got the same warnings as I do about the target. Could you tell me anyone who meets the target?" . . . I said, "Why do they put the target so high?" And they said to me, "Because if they put it lower, the people then will achieve it and they won't have motivation to get more productivity".'

Despite this perpetual state of underachievement, the companies represent some of the most successful global customer-orientated supply chains. In this context, it is difficult to see how workers' performance is correlated to the real logistical performance of a warehouse's operations. In this sense, the tracking of workers contributes to two parallel processes – the actual logistical alignment necessary for the just-in-time distribution of goods into, through and out of a warehouse, and a managerial regime that revolves around ensuring the productivity (and therefore cost-efficiency) of workers.

Nonetheless, it is conceivable that workers could fall foul of what media theorist Matteo Pasquinelli calls 'algorithmic vision'.[26] Highlighting the problem of apophenia within algorithmic governance ('the experience of seeing patterns or connections in random or meaningless data'), Pasquinelli notes, 'There is an excessive belief, indeed, in the almighty power of algorithms, in their efficiency and in the total transparency of the metadata society.' I will return to the idea of the 'almighty power of algorithms' later in this chapter, but the initial implication for workers is that they may have no recourse if managers draw patterns that are not substantiated by reality.

Alongside data communication processes, there are also norms around human communication in the algorithmically mediated workplace. Contrary to the expectations around intellectual and communicative sociality usually found in narratives about the post-Fordist workplace, the overarching norm within algorithmically managed distribution work appears to be towards minimising, either directly or indirectly, communication between workers. 'I never had a job where I talk less,' Lorenzo tells me. 'You talk a bit, like, in the morning or, like, beginning and end of shift, but very minimal. But yeah, never had a job where I talk so little. Yeah, it can be a bit lonely.'

Such reduction of communication is generally felt to be part and parcel of the job. However, direct attempts to minimise verbal communication, particularly by way of supervisory intervention, are also reported. 'You used to be able to talk to people as you went along. Now, and I don't know why, but the team leaders have got a lot more hands on,' Todd explains. 'They will just stand at the end of the aisle and watch you, and if you're talking they'll tell you off for talking.' He says that whether workers are meeting their targets or not seems irrelevant to the managers. 'I had a shop I did the other day: the [items-per-hour target] is 125, I had a big 180-item shop, I got [an] IPH of 250 ... Even if you're getting something like a 200 IPH, they'll still say, "Stop talking, you've got work, don't talk", and stuff like that, so it's fucking like being in the mafia, do you know what I mean? It's like a code of silence. It's really added to the mood of the place.'

While being told not to talk at work is hardly unique to algorithmically managed work, antisociality was widely reported as a feature of it. These rules serve the purpose of directing workers' attention to their personal device, creating an environment where communication is channelled through hardware rather than across the social space of the workplace. 'Often some managers basically shout at you [to stop talking],' says Lorenzo. 'They don't like you to talk because they say you make mistakes when you get distracted and you don't work enough.' Although a by-product of the organisation of work and management rather than its aim, such efforts to reduce unproductive labour time contribute to the intensification of work and imply an affective dimension to the work whereby workers feel isolated from one another. This experience contradicts accounts of computationally dependent work that focus on the increase in cooperative forms of working, and problematises the idea that the increased coordination *of* workers necessitates increased cooperation and communication *between* workers. In Lazzarato's thesis on immaterial labour, he argues:

> if it is no longer possible to lay down and specify jobs and responsibilities rigidly (in the way that was once done with 'scientific' studies of work), but if, on the contrary, jobs now require cooperation and collective coordination, then the subjects of that production must be capable of communication – they must be active participants within a work team. The communicational relationship (both vertically and horizontally) is thus completely predetermined in both form and content; it is subordinated to the 'circulation of information' and is not expected to be anything other. The subject becomes a simple relayer of codification and decodification, whose transmitted messages must be 'clear and free of ambiguity', within a communications context that has been completely normalized by management.[27]

In algorithmically managed distribution work, jobs and responsibilities are still being laid down rigidly, in a broad sense. There is flexibility in the specific tasks being assigned to workers, but any 'cooperation and collective coordination' does not come from the workers being assembled as a team and communicating with each other directly. Rather, it is cooperation and coordination solicited from above, and mediated through 'the system'. There is also some ambiguity in the extent to which workers know they are being coordinated at all. But, to clarify Lazzarato's own ambiguity, it should be made clear that the 'coordination' of jobs pertains to workers being *coordinated* by the management system, rather than *coordinating* themselves.

But Lazzarato does provide an insight into the nature of the communicational relationship, noting that it is 'predetermined in both form and content'.[28] That is to say, communication between workers (horizontally) is mediated through the forms of data communication conveyed (vertically) through the device and management system. As the worker uses their scanner or app, information is relayed both *by* and *to* the worker through predetermined functions within the user interface. We can think of this in terms of the display and the on-screen options the worker interacts with, but also in terms of the constant communication generated by and for the real-time calculations made by the management software to fulfil the dual roles of logistical coordination and performance tracking. Whatever the worker does, or does not do, with regard to the specific tasks assigned to them will therefore generate data in ways over which they have no control. This is the primary mode of communication in algorithmically managed distribution work, which in turn provides the basis for intermittent worker–supervisor communication.

Many of the uses of data tracking, both product- and worker-orientated, could be facilitated by an electronic check-out till. A version of that form of management can be seen at José's Amazon packing station, where his role entails his being stationary at a computer, taking items from a movable wall, scanning and packing them into appropriate boxes, and placing them onto a conveyor belt to be taken to the 'goods out' section. But for mobile distribution workers – especially pickers – algorithmic management entails a particular relation to movement through space.

Warehouse pickers receive locational instructions on a graphic interface attached to a handheld scanner, and their movements are organised through the algorithmic assignment of items. In the case of an Amazon warehouse, the route walked by a picker is planned by real-time calculations which account for the status of orders, as well as the location of stock and other workers. The workload is configured, in the words of architectural theorist Jesse LeCavalier, as 'a continuous process rather than as a goal-oriented sequence', the handheld device acting as the worker's eyes and, to some extent, brain.[29] One result is an altered sense of spatial awareness, the worker not knowing where they are going until they are told to go there – or, in the case of warehouses with tall stacks, having much awareness of where their co-workers or supervisors are at any given time. Spatial disorientation is heightened in an Amazon warehouse, where stock is generally stowed on a random basis. As LeCavalier notes, 'seemingly counterintuitive spatial manifestations appear and are increasingly normalized', because logistical organisation entails a mediation between an abstract (quantitative) environment and a concrete (qualitative) environment that 'enables an imagination that focuses on action rather than form and that measures distance in time'. An artifact of this imagination in the context of Amazon is its random stow system, in which goods brought into the warehouse are stored randomly rather than by category, with the aim of reducing wasted labour time in terms of both pickers' task of searching and the ability to direct workers' movements according to algorithmic calculation. Such a concern for the productive use of movement and the rational use of space may recall the Gilbreths' motion studies; but the key difference is that algorithmic management entails a governance of actions that is not based on 'one best way' which workers can learn or perfect, but a temporally and spatially specific 'one best way' calculated in real time, and incalculable and unknowable to the worker.

Such a system relies on workers effectively being transformed into tracked or 'sensed' entities, along with the stock, via tracking devices.[30] Pickers cannot see the next items they have to collect, so they act solely on the basis of the information displayed on their device. The item queue and their projected work route can then be reprogrammed continuously as they work, without their ever knowing any of the alternative future work patterns they might have been assigned. And yet workers are assessed according to the metrics of a system which is not only unknowable to them, but seemingly unknowable to their human supervisors, too. Moreover, this arrangement has practical effects on workers' own abilities to manage their workload. As Todd explains, in the old system at his online supermarket distribution centre, workers had access to the full 'shop' for their trolley. Therefore, they could employ unsanctioned tricks for making the work physically easier and more mentally stimulating, such as leaving the trolley at the end of an aisle and picking items from shelves using a carrier bag. In the new system, workers cannot see beyond their next item, forcing them to move through the store in more regimented and enforceable ways.

In this way, workers rely on the result of a feedback loop presented to them on their personal interfaces. Instead of an appraisal or evaluation process, an organising role is played by their device, which relays information gathered from their actions that it uses to calculate directives for them without their having to make any decisions for themselves. In this sense, while the handheld scanner carries a literal digital user interface, it also occupies a broader interface position in the sense theorised by Branden Hookway – one that is a moment of alignment or calibration, in this case between physical actions, transmitted signals, databases, algorithms and other processes.[31] The handheld device therefore provides a way into thinking about the live system of symbolic and moving parts of the logistical operation, the system possessing a god's eye view which facilitates the interlocking of discrete processes at a distance.

Here is the frontier of control described by Carter L. Goodrich – the point beyond which 'there shall be no discussion'.[32] At this point, information generated by the worker – whether active, such as that gathered by scanning barcodes, or passive, such as allowing a certain amount of time to elapse between codified device interactions – crosses a threshold as it passes into the system, out of reach of the worker's control or oversight. Practically speaking, workers may be aware of certain points at which their data surfaces, such as on their supervisors' computer monitors. Technically this does not necessarily put the data out of a worker's view; but once it has reached the computers, workers can do little to intervene in its use by a manager or supervisor. When work information is recorded, transmitted and stored digitally on managerial databases, managers have choices about what to do with the data: from updating targets to marking workers for discipline (or 'further training'), from adjusting work allocations via SMS to reorganising the work process altogether.

This characteristic of information technology is what Shoshana Zuboff refers to as *informating*. Along with *automating* certain procedures, she argues that a peculiarity of information technology is that it produces textual information about ('informates') an organisation or work process which was previously beyond the purview of machines.[33] Zuboff argued during the 1980s that the informating capacity of information technology would shatter the Taylorist division of labour by creating, or providing access to, information at the point of production: 'technology returns to the worker what it once took away, with a great deal more as well'.[34] I wish instead to describe an extreme Taylorisation, but one within which the status of management, and managers, is problematised.

As well as the continued development of the material dimension of power, which Zuboff calls 'technique', algorithmic management contains at its heart a rearrangement of authority – as the 'spiritual' dimension of power.[35] I now want to discuss this rearrangement in terms of the elevation of the authority of 'the algorithm' and the subordination of the supervisory function. I want to show that algorithmic management is not just about equipping management with a set of tools collectively referred to as 'algorithms'; rather, it entails a new managerial mode, and with it the production of a new managerial subjectivity. As Jamie Woodcock has noted, there is a question-mark over the degree to which algorithmic management really enhances managerial control, or whether it just provides an illusion of control.[36] By investigating the managerial politics of algorithmic management, we can uncover the character of management in algorithmically managed distribution work.

Algorithmic management relies on the elevation of the status of algorithms within the work process. For workers, this takes two primary forms: first, as social regulation; second, as generative power. This regulative power emerges most obviously in the way performance calculations are leveraged against workers. Whether at team briefings or on the irregular occasions when supervisors approach workers with printouts of productivity scores, the central focus of disciplinary relations between workers and managers is the calculations that the system makes, which are the primary motivator for workers to enhance their performance. But in a further, more technical sense, as the sociologist Scott Lash notes, power is found 'in the algorithm'.[37] Algorithms produce *generative* rules as they function, such as when they 'informate' work, feeding data back into the information workers receive and act upon via their handsets. Circumventing the need for appraisal or traditional learning, control is maintained throughout the system on a more 'protocological' basis, in which software organises information based on the effects it monitors across the digital network and the various moving parts of the labour process without the need for workers' participation as human agents.[38] This process can be observed in simple terms in the way item replacements enacted by workers in Todd's online shopping department affect the future shops of all other workers, without them necessarily knowing that any change has occurred.[39]

These forms of algorithmic authority also destabilise the position of human managers on the shop floor. Like pickers who work without being able to see the next item they will have to collect, supervisors do not have access to the logic of the algorithmic management system either. The pace and scale of the logistical process is too great. Algorithmic management is less a tool for managers to wield as they choose than a system that incorporates everyone on the shop floor – including human managers – and develops its own authority. Although the system produces calculations which may be used by managers against workers, it is not clear to what extent, if any, human managers are themselves involved in the decisions that affect workers. Rather, the algorithms appear as a paternalistic force that commands the obedience not only of workers, but also of supervisors themselves. The main differences between the two groups are the degree to which they are denied knowledge of the managerial process and the political power to enforce discipline. Under algorithmic management, management itself is further divided not only between the 'disciplinarian' and 'executive' (in other words, shop floor and corporate), but between the human and computational.

Many theorists, building on a longer-running discussion within management scholarship about the threat posed by business intelligence systems, have framed this kind of algorithmic management as the automation of management itself. Certainly, the replacement of managers by machines appears to be one dimension of algorithmic management in distribution work, especially where the work is primarily vehicular.

As Lorenzo tells me, 'I didn't see my personal manager, I think, for three months.' Likewise, Noah, one of the Deliveroo riders, hadn't seen a manager in person at all during his time at work – a not uncommon experience. But managers are still involved in the work process even if they are not physically present. The characterisation of algorithmic management as the automation of management therefore fails to tell the whole story. Yes, the use of devices in conjunction with the managerial system means that data is continually collected; but in the algorithmically managed workplace, workers' access to information about the work process is limited. This is a Taylorist move, which aims to put management (rather than labour) in a prime control position, but without requiring the presence of human managers at the site of work. The use of a screen as the first supervisory layer has two key consequences for workers. First, it allows managers to modulate their proximity to the shop floor, making it possible to be physically absent from the work site while computationally present at discrete moments within the work process.[40] Second, the distantiation created by managing workers across a physically distributed network via dispassionate handheld devices allows managers to step behind something of a 'digital veil', providing them with plausible deniability in relation to the commands and calculations of the algorithmic system as a whole. The result is that, while managers are able to distance themselves from the shop floor, the processes of tracking, transmission and performance calculation, and related decisions about task and shift allocation and discipline, are masked by the algorithmic infrastructure. They are therefore 'black-boxed' and made unaccountable. Whereas physical managers can take responsibility and be held accountable for their decisions, even in minor ways, in these workplaces workers must instead, as Todd tells me, simply 'trust the system'. Questioning the system is beyond the reach of human actors. 'There's a phrase at work they keep repeating,' Todd says. ' "Just trust the system". It's, like, quite quasi-religious, to the point where I, like, – "Amen!" – I cross myself when they say it.'

Within these systems, managerial accountability is reduced, and decisions that emanate from the system are not immediately traceable to any particular manager. Instead, they appear ready-formed, to be actioned with limited possibilities for workers to challenge them. Should workers raise concerns with supervisors, as Todd says, they are encouraged to 'trust the system', further asserting the idea that managers themselves are secondary to the strategic vision of impersonal software, and therefore ought not to be judged or held accountable for its judgements. In this sense, *just trusting the system* and managerial distantiation work hand-in-hand. Scrutiny is deflected from human managers towards the non-human management infrastructure, as though human managers were entirely separate from it, merely observers to its mysterious and apparently autonomous workings. Yet we can also observe situations in which the wide reach of algorithmic control does in fact surpass the supervisory abilities of human managers – with increased productivity on the part of workers, there is literally too much information for supervisors to oversee in any meaningful sense. Todd describes how the pace and scale of the work mediated by the system can increase productivity to the point where managers' attention is divided, forcing them to focus on potential bottlenecks arising in the movement of stock rather than the actions of those workers assigned to picking tasks, and therefore creating opportunities for reprieve between shops. As Todd says, 'You gotta remember ... because everybody's doing similar-sized shops, it's never that one trolley will come in at a time, it'll always be twenty at a time ... so, you know, they're rushed off their feet loading these up, getting them organised, getting them ready for the first deliveries at 7 o'clock.' As well as deflecting workers' scrutiny of the system, managers are themselves forced to trust it to some extent.

In Todd's workplace, like the other distribution centres I have discussed, supervisors are still present – their role has not been automated away. But they too are subjected to the use of devices and subordinated to the system. Although basic disciplinary functions remain – commands to stop talking, occasional instructions to work harder – the computational system and its devices wield a technological authority which appears to supersede the authority of the supervisor. Under algorithmic management the supervisory role is modified, putting human supervisors in a peculiar position. Concurrent with the elevation of the authority of the algorithm is an epistemological emptying of the supervisory position. While supervisors retain access to a greater range of devices (such as PCs) and system privileges (such as workers' performance data), their job entails being in service to algorithms as much as overseeing workers. Their role also shifts towards humanistic intervention: although purely intimidatory measures are not precluded, the supervisor may offer 'tips' on how to work more efficiently or introduce novelty features into team briefings such as free pizza, sweepstakes or giveaways interwoven with company communications.[41] José says, 'They try to give you tips how you can go faster. If it works, maybe I could follow the tip. If it doesn't work for me I just find another way. At some points I just get to the conclusion that probably you're not gonna get the target anyway. So I say, "Okay, I follow my ways." Some tips, they help me out, others don't.'

The role is more pastoral than pedagogic. Were it not for their disciplinary powers, we might consider them *subvisors*: they are more subordinated to algorithms than they are placed above workers, among whom their main task is to shepherd cooperation with electronic instructions. The 'quasi-religious' quality of the 'just trust the system' imperative referred to by Todd reflects not only the theological dimension taken on by the system or algorithm, but also the ecclesiastical role adopted by the supervisors, who become, to varying degrees, preachers of the algorithm's sanctity and shepherds of the working flock, themselves subject on all sides to the unknowable calculations of an apparently omniscient power.

The sociologist David Beer describes algorithmic power as embodying 'forms of power that are reactive, concealed, and which are shaped on the ground at the multifarious points of communication'.[42] But algorithmic management also entails a reorganisation of management: while we can see the production of a political phenomenology that affects how workers interact with work and one another both prior to the labour process, while working, in the regulation of communication and in how they experience space, it is also the case that relations of workplace authority are rearranged. Although the supervisory function is reduced in vehicular distribution work (which is arguably a facet of the nature of such work), human managers still play a disciplinary role within distribution centres. But while the algorithmic management system automates aspects of what would historically have been the responsibility of human managers, its 'informating' function means the system emerges as a managerial figure in its own right. Like middle managers in their relationship to more senior human managers, supervisors in the algorithmically managed workplace are on the same 'side' as the system, yet subordinate to it, and working in its service.

These changes in both workers' experience of work and the relations of authority within the workplace are the effects of an extreme Taylorisation facilitated by a real-time algorithmic system, in the context of which we can see a separation of conception from execution, right down to the way workers move through a distribution centre. Heightened computational capacity has resulted in a proliferation of the production and calculation of data, disrupting the role of supervisors. Whereas information about the work process would in the past have been gathered over time or through routine research exercises, the algorithmic management system is based on the real-time production of data as it informates the work process. Concurrently, the conversion of data into directives is largely automated, and can incorporate a far wider range of tracked processes (and at greater speed) than human managers are capable of. While algorithmic management operates within a Taylorist paradigm, it signals a key development in terms of its ability to decentralise the managerial endeavour not by distributing power across the workforce in a more democratic way, but by way of a digital media infrastructure within which real-time cybernetic feedback loops produce a more generative form of control.

Although there is an epistemological hollowing out of both workers and supervisory shop floor management, algorithmic management appears to entail only an ever-greater maximisation of computational knowledge of the work process. Algorithmic management appears to substantiate the autonomist Franco Piperno's claim that

> The central aim of information knowledge is not the completeness and coherence of facts and

judgments on the world, but rather the optimisation of procedures, be they for decisions, diagnosis,
management, or planning. Information knowledge
incessantly transforms procedures so that the action
may be more effective and, above all, faster.[43]

It is not important for workers, or even supervisors,
to retain or expand their knowledge of the productive or logistical process, because 'the system'
produces a continuous present based on calculations that are cast as authoritative and trustworthy.
This logic enables the optimisation of commercial
operations, but it also acts as a technique of managerial power.[44] Others observe that, at Deliveroo,
workers are not provided with an explicit performance target – only an email to say whether they
achieved it or not: a scenario which demonstrates
the fundamental imbalance of knowledge and power
typical of algorithmic management.[45]

The food-delivery platform riders I interviewed
felt that this black-boxing of managerial processes
(in their case within an app) removed the possibility
of certain types of information ever being gained by
workers, to the benefit of management. As Jamie
tells me, 'So, like, if I work as a waiter, I can tell if
I'm needed or not, and if I'm sent home early and
there's no orders I can be, like, "Well, there weren't
any orders, there was no one in the restaurant, to
be fair." Like, obviously it's shit because I should be
guaranteed a wage whatever, but you can kinda see
the demand. Whereas on our end we have no idea
how orders are distributed between riders, whether
that changes over time.' This scenario can be referred
to as 'informational asymmetry', and its presence

within the algorithmic management infrastructure is unsurprising when we consider that asymmetry is both an aim of Taylorism and arguably the condition of human–machine interfaces in general.[46] Nonetheless, this poses significant issues for how we think about the capacity of workers to exercise agency within the work process. In this respect, Lorenzo identifies a key difference between his work at the supermarket distribution centre and the manufacturing job he had moved on to. The distribution centre collected productivity data using bulky digital wristwatches connected to finger-mounted scanners, which was then collated using SAP software.[47] Apart from the times when near-real-time monitors displayed target percentages at the edge of the working area, the day's performance was only known to workers the following morning by way of the shift allocation received by SMS, or when supervisors picked specific workers to approach on the shop floor with SAP printouts. By contrast, performance at the manufacturing job is tracked on a whiteboard that displays twenty to thirty measures of progress relating to various sub-assembly and assembly processes. Figures on the whiteboard are updated every hour or so, and the final figures are assessed at the end of the day. Because the employees are filling in the performance results themselves, they are in possession of productivity information before the manager. As Lorenzo explains, this provides an opportunity for workers to find reasons or excuses as to why the performance took a certain shape before the manager arrives on the shop floor.

One response to the 'blindness' faced by workers within situations of informational asymmetry is to identify the need to improve trust in the way algorithms work.[48] This question was explored by data scientist Min Kyung Lee, who conducted an online experiment to discover participants' perceptions of algorithmic decisions.[49] But it can be seen too in the responses of workers like Jamie and Noah, who feel that the untrustworthiness of the information displayed on their screens (such as the Pulse labour-allocation tool) showed the app giving preference to certain types of workers (moped riders) over others (cyclists) when it came to the allocation of deliveries, harming the prospect of building a sense of common cause between the two groups. However, I am inclined to agree with theorists of internet law Lilian Edwards and Michael Veale that prioritising the 'right to an explanation' is misplaced. Even if this transparency of algorithmic process were granted, there is no guarantee that it would produce the desired effects.[50] In any case, information asymmetry between management and workers need not be a barrier to political action and may in fact offer certain advantages for workplace resistance.

Antonio Negri imagines that 'today, in the post-industrial era, the body and brain of the worker are no longer docile for dressage and horse-training by the bosses; on the contrary, they are more autonomous in building cooperation and more independent from organisational command'.[51] The truth, though, is closer to Mark Fisher's idea. As he writes, 'As production and distribution are restructured, so are nervous systems. To function effectively as a component of just-in-time production you must develop a capacity to respond to unforeseen events, you must learn to live in conditions of total instability.'[52] In recent years the significance of the relationship between management technologies and the development of precarious terms of employment has been strengthened; but even within the confines of distribution workplaces, we can see the emergence of a relationship between a technologically reorganised managerial regime and a political phenomenology of work based on computationally mediated directives and algorithmically enforced performance metrics.

Complementing Zuboff's concept of surveillance capitalism, Waters and Woodcock suggest that algorithmic management can be understood as a 'synthesis of panopticism and Taylorism'.[53] However, although the idea of panopticism may be suggestive of a political will that appears to reflect the motives of algorithmic management, it is far from instructive in explaining the real balance of forces within the work process. To do that, we must also understand algorithmic management as Harry Cleaver suggested – as a strategy that capital must struggle to impose – by enquiring into the political composition of living labour.[54]

6

Guile against Adversity

If you got a job,
you can be an agent.
You can work for revolution
in your place of employment.

— Zounds, 'Subvert'

Strikes may be the primary tool in the arsenal of workplace resistance, but in algorithmic workplaces they are liable to be undermined by the very systems that govern the work. In response, just as the introduction of machines precipitated a need to reorientate working-class organisation from a mode based on workers' technical knowledge and skills towards mass-membership trade unionism, under algorithmic management we can no longer rely on the forms of political mobilisation that have become our common sense. To discover the political mode that is best suited to any organisation of work, we must understand work as a system, as an ecology, and determine where we can leverage power and control within it. Mass strikes are disruptive because they entail a large withdrawal of labour, but in the process there is also a withdrawal of workers' contact with the productive process. But what if a work process was robust or smart enough to fill gaps in labour, or redirect work processes to other locations in real time, even if the barriers to organising strike action were lower than they are? Would we still view strikes as the culmination of workers' power and agency?

If we want to win against the cyberbosses, we will need to think more broadly and creatively than today's trade unions have done. If we can anticipate new directions in algorithmic management, then we also ought to precipitate new directions in workers' political organisation. The natural starting point for this is to consider what actions workers are currently taking against the managerial forms that govern them at work, and to question how these actions can contribute to our understanding of contemporary class struggle in algorithmically organised workplaces.

For some people, any talk of subversion and subterfuge at work is fanciful. It is hard enough to recruit workers to a trade union, or to persuade them to vote for a legal strike. Yet it is no less fanciful than expecting mainstream union negotiators to understand the politics of algorithmic systems better than the bosses who patented them, especially when their own demands are stuck on the thorns of data transparency and AI 'explainability'.

But why not just back unions, or seek to bring about change from inside them? Because the working class itself is more important than its unions as organisations. Trade union membership is a thin metric for understanding the extent of workplace resistance. It's not that unions are unimportant; it's that we should be unsentimental about them. Some unions sanction wildcat strikes or boisterous protests, others clamp down on them. As mentioned in

Chapter 2, GMB was squeezed out of its efforts at Asos by Community after years of resources spent trying to organise workers there, only to do the same thing to IWGB at Deliveroo. Usdaw, a union specialising in representing retail workers, failed to leverage any power against supermarket employers at the time when its workers enjoyed the highest public support, while being subject to the deadliest public health crisis in memory. Large unions like GMB can take the position of being an auxiliary force assisting workers at Amazon while leading a superficial 'partnership' with Uber that effectively denies members a pay-bargaining mechanism. Sure, we can agree that unions are basically good, but there's no political utility in getting misty-eyed about them. What I am interested in is the ability of the working class to struggle; I would like unions to help with that, but history tells us to be prepared for all eventualities.

During the Covid-19 pandemic many people, taking advantage of the technical reorganisation of life and work, found novel ways to skive or slack off at work. In doing so they were able, albeit briefly, to reclaim their time, autonomy and in some cases their dignity, despite the many attempts to monitor their activity.[1] In this chapter I want to explore how workers who are subject to algorithmic control have taken it upon themselves to exploit the organisation of their work to push back against their respective managerial regimes. It's not that I think unionisation is a redundant consideration, but rather that other political forms – which are already being adopted in advance of mass union membership – are seldom examined politically as tactics in their own right.

To judge workplace resistance in terms of its capacity to transform society would be to place an impossible burden upon it; but we can still consider the significance of workplace resistance for those who care about the transformation of class society.[2] As Harry Braverman reminds us, it is imperative that we do not simply accept 'what the designers, owners, and managers of the machines tell us about them.'[3] This also extends to the 'objectivist' view of technologies of organisation taken by trade unions. By extending the principle further, to the political actions of workers themselves, we can see the gap that exists between official efforts to improve conditions in the sector – which either occur outside the workplace, and neglect to focus on the conditions of working life, or take a wholly uncritical view of things like time and motion studies – and the actions being taken by many workers on a daily basis to maximise their interests in spite of efforts by management to mitigate the 'problem' of labour. By neglecting everyday resistance and other forms of 'organisational misbehaviour', we neglect those forms of workplace conflict that do not fit into a rather narrow organising repertoire. Worse still, a failure to see resistance and misbehaviour at work – or diminishing its relevance – preserves the false perception that managers have 'acquired effective techniques of behavioural control'.[4] These are good reasons to reframe the idea of resistance to algorithmic management if we want to develop a political strategy around it. As the labour sociologists Stephen Ackroyd and Paul Thompson argue, the idea that there is now no alternative for workers but total compliance simply does not square with what we know of organisational history, nor with the empirical evidence we have.[5] It also raises the question of what exactly we count as resistance at work.

There are limitations on the term 'resistance', evoking as it does a reactive or negative posture. In this chapter I use it in the way the sociologist Randy Hodson outlines, to refer to acts that are 'intended to mitigate claims by management on workers or to advance workers' claims against management'.[6] Such a definition allows us to shift our focus from a primarily negative stance of refusal towards a more positive conception of struggle. It allows us to think about resistance through the lens of *subversion*. Subversion means we can think about misbehaviour beyond behaviour, resistance beyond negation, and disruption beyond interruption. It allows us to consider action that might take any of these forms, but which might also be understood as an intervention or creative redirection intended to bring about new conditions and to maximise workers' space within the organisation in such a way that they can advance their interests, even for a moment.

It is important to say that workplaces are politically messy places. Resistance does not conform to an ideal type, just as there is no ideal resister. Even the staunchest opponents of managerial regimes can be tangled up in contradictions, ironies and unintended outcomes, while employees often 'consent, cope, and resist at different levels of consciousness at a single point in time'.[7] When politicising resistance we must tread carefully, particularly when workers' actions may not have been undertaken for explicitly ideological ends. As Jamie Woodcock notes, there have been attempts to reframe anything short of complete compliance as sabotage. But whereas sabotage is intended to disrupt crucial mechanisms or machinery, many of the actions we see 'do not significantly undermine the process of capital accumulation'.[8] Nonetheless, they may still be political – if, for example, they are aimed at reappropriating personal dignity robbed by managerial practices.[9]

Less formalised political activity is harder to see, and is not always explicitly ideological. But, while such actions may have a range of motives, this doesn't mean we cannot think about these practices in terms of their amenability to collective action. As Mario Tronti suggested, the breadth, possibility and radical contingency of working-class struggle can be understood as *refusal*.[10] For autonomists, refusal marks 'the beginning of liberatory politics', because it implies the agency of workers within the class relation, particularly the wage-labour relation.[11] In other words, refusal is a key potential arising from the indeterminacy of labour power, the fundamental problem of management. The first radical aspect of refusal, argues Tronti, is that it marks a point of departure from capitalist logic. It is the point at which 'the working class confronts its own labor as capital, as a hostile force, as an enemy', marking not only a point of departure for class antagonism, but a starting point for 'the organization of the antagonism'. Long before we can conceive of revolutionary vehicles for overturning the present state of things, Tronti sees workers' disillusioned, passive non-compliance with work as the spontaneous first step in refusal – the point at which the worker first refuses to be an 'active participant' by 'opting out of the game'.[12] For Tronti, this is fertile ground. 'Hence', he writes,

> what appears as integration of the working class in the system, by no means represents a renunciation of the struggle against capital: It indicates a refusal to develop and stabilize capital beyond certain given political limits, beyond a fixed defensive cordon, from which aggressive sallies can then be launched.[13]

His idea is that the transition from workers' diligent activity to alienated passivity at work is at the same time the beginning of active refusal. The political task is then to overcome passivity by developing 'tactics of organization to actualize the strategy of refusal' – in other words, to collectivise and weaponise refusal beyond its initial spontaneity. This requires an organisational turn that Tronti does less to flesh out, though he does argue that 'passive non-collaboration in the development of capitalism and active political opposition to the power of capital are precisely the starting point and direction of this organizational leap'.

Part of what makes strikes a powerful tool is their visibility: the spectacle of workers together on a picket line. By contrast, most forms of workplace resistance are not actions that workers would want to advertise, especially in insecure workplaces.[14] They can therefore be considered along the lines of Tronti's 'defensive cordon', indicating what the anthropologist James C. Scott calls 'infrapolitics' – 'an unobtrusive realm of political struggle ... That it should be invisible ... is in large part by design – a tactical choice born of a prudent awareness of the balance of power' – but nonetheless grounded in the pursuit of a sort of autonomy.[15] Such acts can appear as both negative forms of action (disengagement; doing a job badly, slowly or uninterestedly) and positive ones (redirecting activity; subversion; denying mediation; 'aggressive sallies'). Both of these constitute forms of everyday resistance that may mitigate managerial efforts or advance workers' claims independently of any official action.

The technical composition of algorithmically managed work is fundamentally cybernetic. It relies on a complex arrangement of interwoven feedback loops which communicate information back and forth between human users and computational components. As I discussed in Chapter 3, the organisation of labour relations across this system is governed by the management interface, which has two aspects. First, it is an architecture of processes – or 'architecture-as-medium', to use Branden Hookway's formulation. Second, it is a threshold that masks and mediates the asymmetry typically represented in the device.

This way of thinking about labour–management relations can help us to understand the effects of resistance upon algorithmic power. It can also illuminate how different types of action affect the cybernetic governance of work, and therefore how workers might establish their own defensive cordons. Resistance *in* the interface disrupts the managerial regime's sense of calibration between logistical processes and factors. The simplest way we can see this type of resistance is in the unintended disruptions that can arise from the technological, practical or social organisation of work. Consider technical malfunctions, which are commonplace in computationally powered workplaces. These can create a blockage to the smooth functioning of the productive process, particularly as workplaces that rely on a functioning digital infrastructure often have no recourse to a non-digital alternative. Moreover, in the downtime created by malfunctions, workers can talk and waste time. We can see one form of this accidental resistance in Lorenzo's distribution centre. There, workers' individual productivity metrics were displayed on TV monitors. But they didn't display everyone's score at the same time, which meant that workers would often huddle around the edge of the grid waiting for their numbers to appear. A measure that had been introduced to boost productivity led to both congestion and wasted time. Meanwhile, conflict between workers themselves often held up the work process, affecting productivity and harming the team spirit that many workplaces aspired to. Sometimes arising from the physical organisation of work (getting in each other's way) or from perceived slights ranging from favouritism to outright racism (particularly in cases of inter-nationality conflict), inter-worker conflict can be viewed as both a failure of human relations management to foster adequately collaborative or amicable working relationships, and as a source of unintended resistance within the optimal functioning of the system.

These moments of accidental resistance reflect resistance as we would expect to find it within an electrical circuit: they hold up the flow of work and – in the case of technological disruption – information that is essential to the algorithmically managed workplace. But they are not what we would typically think of as workers' resistance. Nonetheless, some forms of worker action are functionally similar in terms of their intended resistance in the interface. On Jamie and Noah's food delivery app, for example, a wildcat strike was organised through WhatsApp groups, separate from workers' attempts to unionise (although there would later be wildcat strikes incorporated into union strategy). Workers all agreed to log out of the app at once, scuppering the platform's ability to meet customer demand. While wildcat strikes are typically illegal in Britain, in this case workers used the loophole afforded by their status as independent workers rather than full employees, avoiding any legal consequences. To be effective, the action took advantage of the platform's geography and the nature of its customer demand. Whereas Amazon can re-route parcels to a different fulfilment centre or move delivery slots, a food-delivery platform necessarily operates within a specific locale, covering specific restaurants, and handles time-critical orders with clear peak times. Workers' resistance within the interface is effective due to their being a key part of the digital feedback loop that upholds the continuous logistical process. But the way in which they matter to the system has less to do with what they know or what intuition they have so much as how well they adhere to their device's instructions, as well as the data their work produces. Other forms of resistance in the interface included: obstruction, making someone else's job harder; damage to stock; stealing; wasting time; playing games; making fun of managers; talking; eating; refusing tasks; absenteeism; and, sadly, attempting suicide. Among the most common was testing the limits of what could be considered a good job, with some workers purposefully doing a bad job. José described testing the limits of the automated reporting of late returns from lunch breaks at the Amazon fulfilment centre where he worked. Workers, he claimed, wasted time more liberally once they had concluded that the targets they were expected to meet were unachievable.

Other types of resistance, however, can be said to happen both *in* and *at* the interface. In other words, they challenge the threshold of asymmetry established by the algorithmic governance of the workplace. A key form this might take involves workers taking advantage of handheld devices. 'There are different codes [for when] you made a mistake,' says Lorenzo, gesturing to an imaginary wrist-mounted device. 'What happens is the supervisor has a little barcode that you can scan, then you're out of the productivity counting element. You've got free time, so to speak, to look and see if you made the mistake, if you find the item or whatever that you might have put in the wrong cage.' The possibility of creating time for an unsanctioned break made the code a hot discovery for workers. 'Some workers know the code,' he says. 'I mean, either they've heard it from a supervisor or they have some way to find it out, and the company might change that code because workers use it – you find them in the locker room for five minutes just having a rest, and, you know, okay, they've got the code ... Some of the workers are private with that, because they know if only a few workers have that code it won't [raise suspicions].'

Todd, meanwhile, describes to me the process that workers at his online shopping department had used to exploit their handsets in order to gain unsanctioned breaks. Workers there were able to use a specific button on their scan gun that allowed pickers to remove items above a certain size from their shop, on the basis that the items will not fit on the trolley. But, as Todd explains, when 'you wanna go on your break or you just can't be bothered to push the trolley around anymore because it's really heavy, you'll press that [button] to get rid of the shops to make it go quicker. So you can get away with it, and you can leave or sit down or do something else.' Part of the appeal, for Todd, was that workers who did this could do so anonymously, because customer orders were split across multiple workers' shops. However, after the introduction of a new digital infrastructure, workers were no longer able to determine when their shop would end in this way. Within a week of the new system being introduced, though, Todd had found a workaround. 'With the new system you can't prematurely end a shop,' he explains. 'Now you have to finish the shop before you go on your break or whenever you leave or whatever.' But Todd worked out that switching handsets while logged in gave users the option to make tasks disappear. 'I worked out you could pick up another handset that you're not logged onto ... You log onto it, and then a menu comes up that says "Carry on" or "Exit shop", and if you press the "Carry on" button the shop will switch from this gun to the other gun, which is useful for when you've run out of battery or something like that. Or, if you press the exit, it gets rid of the shop and so you can go on your break again. It puts it back into the system.'

'How easy is it to pick up another gun?' I ask.

'Well, say I take my breaks at 8 o'clock,' he says. 'It's 8 o'clock, and my mate's finished and we're gonna go out for a fag, and she's already logged off her gun. She'll pass me her gun, I'll log onto that. It'll come into the in-between menu where on the other one it's carry on or exit, then exit. So I worked that out the first week the new system was introduced, and the managers didn't know that that could be done – but then they did know about it and I got a bollocking.' I asked how they found out. 'I accidentally went into a really long shop, and I said I'm not gonna do it because I want to go on my break,' he says. '[The team leader] said, "No, you have to do it because you can't come out of a shop." I said, "Yeah, I can', and just did it [laughs]. And yeah, maybe that's how they found out. Grassed myself up. It happens doesn't it?'

In both of these cases, workers exploited cracks in the digital architecture, taking advantage of the organisation of work in order to claim time by outsmarting the system, seizing the opportunity to act outside the gaze of supervisors and engage in limited forms of collaboration with other workers. In Lorenzo's case, workers were able to resist the claims of the productivity system – in particular, the intensity demanded by the maintenance of the cases-per-minute rate, the length of time between breaks, and the exclusivity of the code itself, which was reserved for supervisors and managers. Until the change of system, Todd was able to take breaks from working with relative freedom by using the 'item will not fit' button; and until he made his team leader aware of the workaround he had discovered, he and his colleagues had been able to re-establish control over their break times by using the handset-switching technique. Workers thereby took advantage of the physical distantiation of managers, as well as their trust in the algorithmic management system, both in terms of its ability to keep workers working and its capacity to reflect periods of downtime in its performance calculations. As a form of resistance, it allowed workers to suspend the workflow by disrupting the data transmission between their device and the system, enabling them to move around the workplace as they wished in order to take breaks on their own terms.

But at Lorenzo's distribution warehouse, workers were able to intervene in the workflow itself, as a result of a slowdown conducted by agency workers during one shift. Having begun organising through a series of after-work meetings, the agency workers formulated a set of demands that included pay parity with in-house workers and guaranteed shifts. Temporary agency workers were being paid just 70 per cent of what in-house staff were paid for the same job. To protest against this, and in the hope of securing a minimum number of shifts per week, they aimed to reduce their productivity to 70 per cent of what was specified in their targets. The action was conceived by non-union salts (politicised workers who join a workforce in order to organise within it) but was joined by an initial group of supportive workers, before spreading to include most of the agency workers on-shift. The scale of adoption was partly spontaneous: a successful gamble on the part of those who had initiated the action. The slowdown was planned as a one-day protest in support of a set of demands formulated by a group of around ten temporary workers at the warehouse. A central part of it was the relationship between the productivity rate and the system of shift allocation via SMS. The conception, execution and aftermath of the action was relayed to me by Lorenzo.

'We had political aspirations,' he begins. 'We thought, okay, we have to first of all break the system of shift allocation and productivity rate . . . as long as they allocate the shifts as they want and tie it to the productivity rate, it will be like a rat race . . . So we said, okay, we want four shifts guaranteed at least per week, never mind the productivity rate.'

'The main discussions were amongst us [working] in the grids, and we said, okay, what is our possibility?' he explains. The group agreed they would read out their demands in the morning briefing, before holding a day-long slowdown, working at 70 per cent of productivity. 'We work 70 per cent because we only get 70 per cent,' he continues. 'So a basic kind of equation.'

'The permanent workers were not included. Maybe that was a mistake, or maybe it was good because maybe they would have talked,' he says. 'About three-quarters of the temps took part, and you could see productivity going down. People were having fun. For one or two hours it was real fun, because you could really see everyone is working slow and making fun of it, going slow-motion, and you could see the supervisor coming in to have a meeting with [the logistics company] and [saying], "What are you doing? What the fuck?"'

'So, for two hours it was really great, and then they asked the permanent workers to work over-time, and they did – maybe also because some of them were not even aware that there was something like an "action" going on . . . We talked to them a bit, but also we didn't want to be too vocal. In the end we were too vocal . . . We got a disciplinary and we got kicked out, and yeah, that was it.'

The slowdown was conceived as an intervention against one of the primary political forms taken by management: the mechanism which tied agency workers' productivity to their daily shift allocation. The organising group took advantage of the daily briefing to publicise their demands and relied on the proximity of workers on the grid for other temporary workers to join in with the action. Notably, the action made use of and subverted workers' experience of the digital infrastructure of the productivity system. Workers, being used to finding out their productivity percentage on a day-to-day basis by SMS, were able to subvert their embodied relationship with the workflow to achieve the desired rate of effort – 70 per cent of target productivity – which was confirmed in the following day's messages. The slowdown was also fun. It intervened in the usual psychosocial dynamic of the work by flouting and subverting the authority of the algorithmic system, thereby making visible the illusion of managerial control and its reliance on workers' cooperation.[16]

Although the slowdown was unsuccessful, it was an attempt to push back openly against poor pay, worker competition, unforgiving productivity management and the SMS shift-allocation system. The threat of that system was also resisted through the slowdown, workers appearing to set aside concerns about the direct effect their participation would have upon their own shift allocation. Meanwhile the action advanced claims both overt and implicit: overt in the case of the pay and shift-allocation demands; implicit in the case of inter-worker cooperation and collaboration, and in subverting the authority of the productivity system by second-guessing its calculation.

Further along the supply chain, Todd was advancing his own claims against the managerial regime in his supermarket, albeit covertly, by making intentional mistakes. This took two main forms: performing product relocations incorrectly, which confused the database and led to stock errors; and abusing the substitution function on the handheld device in order to sabotage the stock database, which is updated according to workers' inputs. Some amusement was also provided by giving customers incorrect items of the worker's choosing; the bottleneck created by the organisation of shops meant that supervisors were unable to check whether the substitutions were appropriate. Although there is a clear incentive to cut corners on a product relocation if it will negatively affect one's productivity calculation, Todd was intent on identifying new methods of refusal with little discrimination: 'You're bored out your nut . . . it's very low-paid work, and just for the sake of my self-esteem here, Craig, I want to make it feel like I'm being valued. I want to make my work as expensive as possible by being as least productive as possible. The less work I do in the hour, the more that little bit of work that I've actually done is worth. So for the fact of self-esteem I want to make that £7.80 stretch out a bit. So, yeah, away from the sarcasm, it's bitterness. You'll kick out at the boss, at the job, for being shit. It can make the job fun. One of my favourite things to do at the moment is – because they can't see who's substituted things, there's no drawback, no backlash you're gonna get – every single film or DVD that gets requested, I substitute for *Star Wars: Rogue One*, because it's a sick film and everyone should see it. Yeah, just stuff like that. It's funny – it's fun to do.'

I ask whether managers might be able to work out who had made the substitution, if they could look at the records. 'I'm not sure if they can or they can't,' he tells me. 'But I've been repeatedly substituting things like *Peppa Pig* for *Rogue One*. Someone ordered a TV boxset of something, got given *Rogue One* instead. So it's really obvious, like this is not even a connected item.' No manager had ever spoken to Todd about the substitutions, however far they deviated from the original order, suggesting they didn't have oversight of that part of the workflow. 'They can see the substitutions are happening, because they can see what buttons you pressed,' he says. 'But they don't seem to be able to see what's been substituted for what, just that a substitution's taken place . . . It seems to suggest that the shopper is made anonymous. I don't know how far it can be pushed. It's something I'm still trying to figure out.'

As Todd admits, the work is infantilising, making workers, especially young workers, want to play up. Regardless of his tone, Todd was expressing an active dissatisfaction, and establishing for himself what he felt was a defensive cordon against the more onerous claims placed upon workers by management. In doing so, he was attempting to mitigate the perceived punitive nature of the work, the authority and paternalism of digital instructions, and what Todd considered to be the demeaning character of the work – especially the boredom it induced. He was thereby able to sabotage the informating aspect of the algorithmic management system by sending false information across the algorithmic threshold, taking advantage of managerial distantiation and the communication options afforded by the handsets in order to make fun, get pleasure from insubordination and possibly inflict reputational damage on the company.

The workers I spoke to often referred to their understanding of what the supervisors could or could not know about them from the other side of the threshold of the interface. This understanding was informed partly by the disciplinary consequences that arose, but also by multiple efforts to see what supervisors were seeing on their computers. 'I saw the opportunity to have a look at the screen,' Todd says of one such occasion. 'I said to the manager, "I don't understand. What do you mean?" And she said, "No, it's all up here on the screen." She showed me [the computer], and it had a list of every single button that had been pressed.' But Lorenzo adopted a more skirmish-like approach. In his warehouse, the workers would wait for supervisors to be in a different part of the building before logging into their PC. 'Workers know how to operate a computer,' he tells me. 'Normally you're not supposed to touch it, but there is, for the supervisors, a computer at the end of the grid and some workers who have been there a bit longer, they know how to get [into it]. So if they want to know about their productivity rate they can look it up on the supervisor's computer.'

By taking advantage of the layout of the workplace, or indeed of the supervisors themselves, these actions intervene in managerial political forms to gain insight into the other side of the algorithmic frontier. Such snooping allowed access behind the curtain of the management interface, through which workers could advance a claim to knowledge of their own performance and the asymmetrical functioning of the system more broadly. For Lorenzo, this was largely a question of assessing whether or not workers had been overworking, whereas for Todd it arose from a broader concern about the actions workers could get away with. In both cases, workers resisted the assumption of the managerial retention of data generated by workers, in terms of both the range of data points and the content of the data.

Taking advantage of handheld devices, holding a slowdown, making intentional mistakes and snooping are creative forms of refusal and subversion that demonstrate an intimate and intelligent understanding of the workplace. They show an awareness of the importance of the architecture of processes underpinning algorithmic management, as well as an awareness of the asymmetrical struggle over information that is represented in the interface. For this reason, they offer a different way of thinking about workers' resistance to algorithmic governance on the shop floor.

Lorenzo contrasted the ability to tamper with figures in his most recent job, where productivity is calculated manually on a whiteboard by workers, with his earlier work at the distribution warehouse, where productivity data was collected and processed digitally. The non-digital aspect of reporting allows workers to ensure they are achieving satisfactory targets fairly easily, even if in fact they fall short. Working within an algorithmic productivity system, on the other hand, had forced him and his colleagues to be more inventive in their approach.

A key tool for the group of workers who initiated the slowdown was a printed workplace bulletin. Authored by workers from different sites with a view to organising, these bulletins were generally handed out at break times, between jobs, or before or after work. They typically contained details of exploitative practices within the workplace and information about related workplaces, or workers organising politically in other parts of the company (whether at a different site or in a different country). But they had also flagged particular workers for disciplinary processes once they took action at work.

Jamie and Noah said that riders for the delivery platform relied heavily on WhatsApp to organise themselves, yet once managers became aware of this they viewed participants with suspicion. In one case, managers reportedly infiltrated a staff WhatsApp group and used it to discipline an employee marked out as an agitator, before contriving to scupper a planned union meeting by holding a rival meeting at the same time with a voucher incentive for attendees. For this reason, other organisers opted instead to set up Facebook pages, which could act as a one-to-many medium for announcements, but also as a one-to-one medium through direct messages with workers.

Such practices are considered 'bread and butter' methods for recruiting fellow workers, and are deployed by large, small and unincorporated worker organisations the world over. By contrast, some acts of informal resistance might superficially be dismissed as selfishness, laziness or carelessness – indeed Lorenzo, while relaying details of some of these tactics, lamented their apparent individualism. But they nonetheless occupy an important place within the frame of resistance, not least because they form by far the largest category of such acts among those I was told about. Moreover, they force us to think about resistance beyond what is familiar, despite in most cases their familiarity. In a way, it is less the strategic effectiveness of such actions that represents a challenge than the way in which they are perceived. Should we assume that anything outside union-sanctioned action is surplus to the plan, and is perhaps even something to side with managers on – as trade unions sometimes do? Or should we take such actions as clear evidence of an untapped reservoir of feeling that we should seek to harness?

Whatever our prejudices about informal forms of resistance might be, such tactics are not accidental, and are almost always the result of what Braverman refers to as 'active dissatisfaction'.[17]

An obvious objection to any attempt to politicise these actions is that they are largely those of disgruntled individuals, or at least individuals intent on finding ways to be disruptive – though this does not negate their political content, even if their scope seems marginal. But it is an open question whether these individual actions and others like them have the capacity to be scaled up or generalised across a workforce as part of a collective endeavour. This was a point of reflection for both Lorenzo and Todd. They highlighted that many tactics might be considered 'individual ways to deal with the system', and expressed concern about a lack of 'collective feeling'. But, at the same time, both saw their tactics as ones that will be learned 'if you've worked there long enough', and recognised that rendering managerial political forms 'useless' relies on such tactics becoming 'common practice'.

With this in mind, we need to abstract from the observable moments of resistance to consider the principles they evoke. As Thompson and Ackroyd argue, 'The essential conditions for resistance and misbehaviour are still present . . . It is not a case of "waiting for the fightback", romanticising the informal, or disregarding the capacity of unions to renew their own organisation and strategy.' Our job is to 'put labour back in, by doing theory and research in such a way that it is possible to "see" resistance and misbehaviour, and recognize that innovatory employee practices and informal organisations will continue to subvert managerial regimes.'[18]

Common to these forms of resistance is something we could call *metis*, after the Ancient Greek term μῆτις, denoting the application of a form of knowledge which is variously practical, situated, cunning, experiential, wily, vernacular and deceptive.[19] Like the actions themselves, the term is slippery, but today it is usually interpreted as 'cunning intelligence'. While it is often reduced to the idea of local knowledge, responsive intelligence, know-how or knack, design strategist Benedict Singleton makes the case that a fuller and more accurate understanding of the term requires the inclusion of duplicity and guile.[20] In a classic text on the subject, the historians of ancient Greece Marcel Detienne and Jean-Pierre Vernant describe the term as a way of knowing which 'implies a complex but very coherent body of mental attitudes and intellectual behaviour which combine flair, wisdom, forethought, subtlety of mind, deception, resourcefulness, vigilance, opportunism, various skills, and experience over the years'.[21] Resistance or refusal involving metis is active. Metic resistance is not merely a drag on workflow, but an intervention into the system itself. Think of the slowdown whose aim was to reduce the performance rate to a specific level to make a point about pay disparity. Rather than merely working more slowly than usual, participants had to gauge their work rate based on experiential intelligence and judgement. Metis emphasises the dimension of refusal that is not merely withdrawal, but rather the inventive action of conducting one's time and energy to reorientate labour time towards one's own will, against the efforts of the managerial endeavour. To understand resistance as metic is to evaluate the notion of 'doing what you're not supposed to' so as to draw out the practical and situational acumen that informs such actions, as well as affirming the agency of the people who undertake them. Resistance in this sense is a subversion (and reappropriation) of one's own labour – a reorientation of activity towards satisfying one's own preferences and getting away with it.

As Woodcock notes, it can take some time before workers feel comfortable enough at work to begin engaging with other workers, especially for the purposes of deviating from managerial instructions, because of the initial fear of being sacked.[22] What in the end makes the worker feel comfortable enough to talk on the job and exploit opportunities for non-work activity is what Lorenzo and Todd refer to when describing their tactics for pushing back against managerial systems: the learned knowledge of where those opportunities exist, and how to get away with taking advantage of them. This is metis in action.

Tactical intelligence, in this sense, is opportunistic. As Michel de Certeau argued, tactics constitute the art of 'tricking' order against itself.[23] Lacking the strategic power afforded by a proper locus – such as a place outside the relentless workflow – the art of playing tricks in this way 'involves a sense of the opportunities afforded by a particular occasion' which invokes a 'clever utilization of time' – and indeed a sense of *kairos* (καιρός), or the 'right' time, and a 'sense of the opportunities' to pull a tactic off successfully. Metic resistance is necessarily political rather than technical. This is what Frederick Winslow Taylor recognised early in the twentieth century when he observed workers' ability to regulate the productivity of their work, and thus the ratio of effort to wages.[24] Taylor's response was similarly political; but, despite the spread of scientific management methods into algorithmic management systems, metic subversion persists.

This can also be seen in anxieties about Uber drivers failing to cooperate with the app by 'gaming' it.[25] But whereas Uber relies on a decentralised standing reserve of unpaid would-be workers, workers in distribution centres are tracked within a productivity system for the large majority of their working hours. In these workplaces, the cunning required in resistance involves learning or experimenting with what the management system and human managers can and cannot know. As Todd puts it when questioned about managers' ability to find out about his purposefully inappropriate swapping of items, 'They don't have time to check through 160 boxes with the sheet of paper with all of this, so you take advantage of the lack of manpower.'

Taking advantage of the supervisory reliance on visual checking was likewise reported in Woodcock's ethnographic observations of call centre workers, who would reset their timers to claim a few extra minutes for their break.[26] But, as we saw in the previous chapter, managerial reliance on the algorithmic system sits alongside managerial distantiation and alters the ways managers maintain their presence and control over workers. Such a system requires a measure of cooperation on the part of workers, at the very least in terms of the communication demanded by their handheld devices. Todd made use of informational refusal or subversion, whereby the data given to the system was in the correct form but was false or misleading. With managers largely absent from the shop floor, workers instead 'negotiate' with the interface or system, which – being designed to anticipate compliant workers – is unable to respond in comparably cunning ways. This is what has been called a 'counter-logistical moment'.[27]

Contemporary activist responses to the organisation of the distribution sector and the phenomenon of logistics often focus on the possibility of locating leverage – or 'fault lines and weak points', as the Transnational Social Strike Platform puts it – where workers might concentrate power to tip the balance of control in their favour.[28] Logistics acts as a fulcrum within the wider economy, and such a strategy is an attempt to use this to the advantage of workers. As a strategy, however, it falters against the scale of managerial control. This forces many organisers to settle on the contractual aspects of working conditions as a predicate for effective future action. But, as we have seen, there is little to stop companies simply discriminating against workers. Metis gives us a way of thinking about leverage more precisely. Singleton argues that levers conceptually embody metis because they manipulate physical circumstances to move greater weights with smaller forces, against apparent probabilities.[29] This is one reason Plato spoke so scathingly of metis when it first came under philosophical scrutiny: he saw the shrewd machinations of traps, which allowed the small to capture the strong, as a form of sophistry compared with the nobility and, in his view, truthfulness of the traditional hunt. Applied to the workplace, what emerges from an application of metis is a form of workers' power that looks more like *workers' guile*: the use of situated wisdom and experiential cunning to seize or subvert, even momentarily, the current of managerial control – 'to create and expand the glitches in the system'.[30]

If our starting point is always managerial claims over the work process, it is tempting to be lured into an account of resistance that can only set out from a negative posture, in which we ask *what is left* for resistance when managers have thought of all the ways they might discipline, incentivise, control, persuade and curtail workers away from anything but productive compliance. But such a position takes ideal managerial types at their word, and ignores the point that the introduction of a new technology can never be fully planned, and that, from a strategic perspective, this approach offers vanishingly little in terms of assessing the potential for workers to exercise autonomy, which – as the examples above show – is worked out in practice over time.

As we know, managerial, and indeed governmental, interventions have long sought to curtail or control collective action. Nevertheless, we see the endurance of resistance in the workplace. By looking at actually existing workplaces, we can see that workers are never fully subsumed. While formal modes of collectivism might be elusive, there remains what we might call a commons that is present in even the individual acts of insubordination that comprise a shared situational understanding and knowledge, based on the hidden transcript of the workplace.[31]

Resistance within and at the interface seldom arises from the lone ingenuity of a single individual. Even in cases where that interpretation is closer to the truth, workers have relied on the complicity of their colleagues to remain undetected. While resistance may, in one sense, take the form of individual acts of refusal, in another it is embedded within a social situation that provides their conditions of possibility. This may involve inducting other workers into the tricks they can deploy at work, or simply ignoring the misbehaviour of others.

This is the basis of everyday resistance. Understanding of and access to these commons cannot be deduced by sorting through the various formal managerial claims over workers. It takes time to emerge. It does not reside only in the gaps between steps in a process, but in a disposition developed within and between workers over time. It is a workplace counterculture that workers develop through interaction with one another and their surroundings. This is the difference between new workers, who are scared to deviate from what is expected of them, and the worker who knows what they can get away with. This culture is not readily accessible to managers, no matter how many *gemba* walks they take. Moreover, it cannot be researched without inquiring into the daily lives of workers. As an anonymous supermarket worker wrote for the British communist group, Plan C:

The first few weeks you assume everyone's a jobs-worth. You feel watched all the time. But after three months you stop giving a shit and start to slack off. Then you notice other people slacking off in the same way as you. You bump into someone by the bailing machine and give them a knowing smile as you get your phone out. It's never explicit, but after six months you give each other the look; 'I know you've just been doing fuck all for the last half hour, good on you.' Then you get close to people, and try and one up them on how much shit you have or haven't done. 'We once took 40 minutes for a 15 minute break but got fucking dobbed in by Mary'.[32]

In laying out the rationale for his *Principles*, Taylor was concerned about the transferral of resistance tactics from older to younger employees. In this, he recognised the commons shared between workers which creates the possibility of autonomy.[33] One reason for Taylor's recommendations to companies to break down tasks into simpler units was to disrupt the shared infrapolitical realm that exists at the level of metis among workers. What charges of individualism miss about informal action is that these tricks and tips are often transferred between workers, creating chains of discovery through the workforce. Even where they are not, we can still say some forms of resistance are generalised, in that they are regularly enacted by workers from day to day – they might not be acting *for* their class, but they are still in a sense acting *as* a class, with due political significance.

By thinking about resistance in terms of metis, we are forced to consider the situatedness of political action away from ideal types, such as those found in the organiser's repertoire. While this may be advantageous to workers, in that it elides managers, it also presents political challenges. Where the notion of the commons allows us to think about the social prerequisites for political action, metis encourages us to consider the space of the labour process, as well as the forms of social organisation and social knowledge arising from the phenomenological reality of working in particular workplaces. The resister must be seen as a cunning and intelligent actor, an active agent implicated in the infrapolitical realm. But, more than this, the lens of 'metic commonality' forces us to think about where collectivity and organisation already exist. As Woodcock writes,

At the start of each three-and-a-half-hour shift there was a buzz session with the supervisors . . . The length of the buzz session was never officially defined and therefore it was at the discretion of the supervisors. This meant that as long as the games or discussion continued it could be stretched out. This involved a level of informal organisation as one individual worker could extend the session by asking more questions as the supervisors would catch on that they were trying to distract them and therefore cut the buzz session short. A successful extension involved a careful balancing act of feigning interest, posing questions and stimulating discussion . . . a collective approach emerged around this. Subtle cues would be exchanged under the gaze of the supervisors, a nod or raise of the eyebrows encouraging others to participate in the process. Although even the best attempts – which

were then gleefully relayed to others in the breaks –
could delay the start of work by at the most
forty-five minutes, it was viewed as a significant
victory.[34]

Here we see the trial and error of repeated buzz
sessions, the shared social understanding between
workers, the political desire to reclaim time and
have fun, and the metic creativity of inventing reasons to keep the sessions going. In the examples I
have given, we can consider the exploitation of
menu options to bring about breaks; the stealing
and sharing of supervisors' codes or computer
log-in details; use of the knowledge of what supervisors can and can't know, and how busy they will
be at a given moment, to amuse oneself and create
problems for the stock database; defiance of the
narrow forms of communication demanded by
interfaces; the shared experience invoked in slowing down to 70 per cent of productivity, reasserting
workers' autonomy over performance; the ingenuity of testing new equipment in order to find new
ways to subvert it – and all the lessons passed
between workers through these actions, the blind
eyes turned and the sense of empowerment felt.
We see confirmed in acts of metic commonality the
illusion of the extent of managerial control, a 'precarious assemblage' exposed by workers' guile.

Within the algorithmically managed workplace,
metic commonality manifests itself as a sort of tactical shrewdness that grasps the way computational
structures intersect with the human dynamics of the
work setting.[35] The examples given here make use
of the way algorithmic management affects work

and rearranges authority. Managerial distantiation, for example, represents a clear opportunity for metic commonality to emerge, operating under the algorithmic radar, carving out space between tracking and action in the knowledge that managers will first and foremost trust the system. For this reason, metic commonality brings a different sort of asymmetry to the management interface, which all workers might potentially have access to.

The tactics I have outlined in this chapter are real tactics that are being explored by workers. They can therefore help us see resistance more clearly where it is not immediately obvious. They are defensive cordons from which workers can advance claims to time, dignity and autonomy. Such a view is very different to that of trade unions. The warehouse workers I spoke to were generally indifferent to their own trade unions – and, while the legal battles being fought by unions are significant, their focus covers only a small part of workers' grievances, and their irrelevance to large sections of this chapter is indicative of their general lack of presence in shop floor struggles. As things stand, unions lack whole swathes of knowledge of the workplaces they wish to represent; and, while they may have all but abandoned the struggle over the labour process, workers in those workplaces have not, even if their actions are often undertaken covertly. While technologies of management are intended to curb and direct worker (mis)behaviour and extend control to every corner of the workplace, worker resistance demonstrates guile against adversity, displaying cunning intelligence to re-thread power and technology against management.

Epilogue

Find each other.
— The Invisible Committee

At the time of writing, Hollywood is shut down, as the Writers Guild of America West strike enters its fourth month. Against the background of the deep changes initiated by the rise of streaming on film and TV distribution, the union is demanding better pay and residuals, as well as assurances around the staffing of American writers' rooms. Yet headlines have been dominated by one issue more than any other: artificial intelligence.

AI means different things in different contexts, but it has inarguably entered the zeitgeist. This is partly due to ChatGPT, a large language model that uses as its dataset a vast amount of written content from the surface web. But its presence extends to the height of pop culture – it is even the villain in the latest *Mission: Impossible* film – as well as its nadir – in the new trend for 'deep fake' pornography. The apparent flexibility of AI, as well as the speed of its development, is worrying. So it is unsurprising that, when applied to an industry we typically think of as being defined by its humanity – creative writing – whose product constitutes a significant portion of culture itself, many fear its potential effects. But although large language models are uniquely placed to threaten writing professions, part of AI's cultural appeal is its familiarity: it is an updated version of the robots coming for our jobs.

Many labour commentators and film journalists have been quick to note how unlikely it is that AI will replace writers altogether. AI doesn't have childhood trauma, as one viral placard put it. But it could 'gig-ify' writing work. In this scenario, writers – especially junior writers – might be hired to rework AI-drafted scripts, or conversely write drafts for AI to redraft. Others might even be hired to front AI-generated work, undermining other writers in the process. The issue is less about automation than labour control, in what is a highly unionised industry.

The WGA's demand on AI is the simplest of all its positions: 'Regulate use of artificial intelligence on [minimum basic agreement]-covered projects: AI can't write or rewrite literary material; can't be used as source material; and MBA-covered material can't be used to train AI.'

In a word, its demand is for suppression.

Compare this to Britain's Trades Union Congress, whose *AI Manifesto* hinges on 'explainability' and human connection, as does the White House's *Blueprint for an AI Bill of Rights*. Compare this also to the American Strategic Organizing Center's Amazon campaign, which is fixated almost exclusively on health and safety as the basis for contesting its managerial regime, as in Britain. 'There's a really deep set of labor movement issues involved in just ensuring that algorithmic management systems actually follow the law,' Amanda Ballantyne, director of the AFL-CIO's Technology Institute, told *Politico*, 'that there's openness, accountability, and a worker's voice in the way that those systems are implemented.'[1]

As Raniero Panzieri would have put it, these are typically objectivist positions. Whatever concerns they convey, they are predicated on a dutiful acceptance of the application of technological innovation to workers. But, as I argued at the beginning of this book, both transparency and health and safety are thin ledges upon which to hang our concerns. When we talk about technology, what we are really talking about is the organisation of work. Unfortunately, despite the clear urgency of the situation, many unions remain distracted by an imaginary future in which we get to share the benefits of automation with bosses despite the wealth of evidence showing they do not share such a vision.

Nor should it be ours. In campaigning for the suppression of AI, the WGA has found itself far in advance of the rest of the trade union movement, because the particularities of its industry lay bare the implications of the technology. Large language models are not a health-and-safety risk, and neither transparency nor 'explainability' will make them more equitable. Likewise, any suggestion of 'sharing the benefit' of AI is quickly undermined by the reality of the existing pay disparity between studios and writers. The WGA has understood what other unions ought to learn: the infeasibility of leaving technology within the realm of corporate decision-making.

Acknowledgements

This book was written in Harehills, Leeds, alongside my day job over the course of a couple of challenging years. Constants in this time have been my rescue dog, Bella; my dear friend Sarah Jaffe, who has been an unwavering source of support both personally and professionally; and a seemingly immortal group chat called Thread. I'm immensely grateful to them all, in different ways.

I would like to thank John Merrick, my editor, whose insight has been invaluable, and everybody who has worked on the publication of this book at Verso. I would also like to thank Clare Hymer, Nicole Aschoff and Aaron Bastani for their encouragement in the early stages of writing, and Nick Srnicek and Grace Blakeley for some very helpful phone calls when the book was still a proposal. I would also like to express my sincere appreciation to Steve Lake and Zounds for allowing me to reproduce the lyrics of their song 'Subvert'.

Writing this book would not have been possible without the patience of my colleagues at Novara Media and numerous friends who have shown me love. I have not taken it for granted. Further back, Nate Tkacz has been a vital champion of this project since 2014, and I would also like to thank Celia Lury, David Berry and Phoebe Moore for their guidance. I'm also indebted to Seth Wheeler, whose political insights are infused throughout the work.

In the final leg of writing, I have been ridiculously fortunate to count on the love and enthusiasm of Amanda Wowk. Thank you.

Finally, I am sincerely grateful to every worker I spoke to over the course of this project, as well as all their comrades and allies. Any mistakes are my own, and any ingenuity theirs.

Notes

1 The Stakes

1. Carter L. Goodrich, *The Frontier of Control: A Study in British Workshop Politics* (London: Pluto, 1975), p. 3.
2. Ibid., p. 56.
3. Nick Dyer-Witheford, *Cyber-Proletariat: Global Labour in the Digital Vortex* (London: Pluto, 2015), p. 39.
4. Sarah O'Connor, 'When Your Boss Is an Algorithm', *Financial Times*, 8 September 2016.
5. Adam Barr, 'Microresistance: Inside the Day of a Supermarket Picker', *Notes From Below*, 20 March 2018, at notesfrombelow.org.
6. Mark Fisher, *Capitalist Realism: Is There No Alternative?* (Winchester: Zero, 2009), p. 80.

2 Algorithmic Work

1. See Craig Gent, 'When Logistics Run Out of Time', *Novara Media*, 23 March 2020, at novaramedia.com.
2. *Newsnight*, BBC, 19 March 2020.
3. Kim Moody, *On New Terrain: How Capital Is Reshaping the Battleground of Class War* (Chicago: Haymarket, 2017).
4. *Panorama*, 'Amazon: The Truth Behind the Click', BBC, 25 November 2013; *Channel 4 News*, 'Workers "Treated Like

Scum" in the JD Sports "Prison" Workhouse', 12 December 2016; Sara Spary and Laura Silver, 'The Real Cost of Asos's Fast Fashion', *BuzzFeed News*, 29 September 2016, at buzzfeed.com.

5. Min Kyung Lee, Daniel Kusbit, Evan Metsky and Laura Dabbish, 'Working with Machines: The Impact of Algorithmic, Data-Driven Management on Human Workers', *Proceedings of the ACM/SIGCHI Conference on Human Factors in Computing Systems* (2015), at dl.acm.org. See also Alex Rosenblat and Luke Stark, 'Algorithmic Labor and Information Asymmetries: A Case Study of Uber's Drivers', *International Journal of Communication* 10: 27 (2016), pp. 1603–12.

6. Jörn Boewe and Johannes Schulten, *The Long Struggle of the Amazon Employees: Laboratory of Resistance* (Brussels: Rosa-Luxemburg-Stiftung, 2017), pp. 27–9. See also Gregor Gall, 'Union Busting at Amazon.com in Britain', *Indymedia UK*, 21 January 2004, at indymedia. org.uk.

7. Boewe and Schulten, *Long Struggle*.

8. . . . ums Ganze! 'G20 Hamburg: Blast the Chain. Bring the Harbour to a Halt.' *Plan C*, 2017, at weareplanc.org. See also *NBC News*, 'Occupy Disrupts Pacific Ports; Arrests in Seattle, NYC, Houston', 12 December 2011.

9. Sarah Butler and Hilary Osborne, 'Courier Wins Holiday Pay in Tribunal Ruling on Gig Economy', *Guardian*, 6 January 2017. See also GMB @ Asos, 'Asos – Respect Your Workers!', 2016.

10. See Craig Gent, 'How Do We Solve a Problem Like Amazon?', *Novara Media*, 27 November 2020, at novara media.com.

11. Some workplaces have been anonymised by agreement with the workers I spoke to about them. This is to protect workers' identities and, in some cases, to enable them

to discuss their views and actions without fear of recrimination from their employers. For the same reasons, I have also changed workers' names throughout.

12. Phoebe V. Moore, *The Quantified Self in Precarity: Work, Technology and What Counts* (London/New York: Routledge, 2018), p. 3.

13. Jesse LeCavalier, *The Rule of Logistics: Walmart and the Architecture of Fulfillment* (Minneapolis: University of Minnesota Press, 2016), pp. 1–30.

14. Udit Madan, Michael E. Bundy, David D. Glick and John E. Darrow, 'Augmented Reality User Interface Facilitating Fulfillment', 2018, US Patent 2018/0218218 A1.

15. Although moped riders do have higher hourly averages, they also tend to work longer shifts than cyclists.

16. Harry Braverman, *Labor and Monopoly Capitalism: The Degradation of Work in the Twentieth Century* (New York/London: Monthly Review, 1974), p. 10.

17. In 2016, 129,000 days were lost to the BMA's junior doctors' strike. See Office for National Statistics, 'Labour Disputes in the UK: 2016', 2017, at ons.gov.uk.

18. Labour Market Analysis, *Trade Union Membership 2016 Statistical Bulletin* (London: Department for Business, Energy and Industrial Strategy, 2017).

19. As Nick Dyer-Witheford has highlighted, the decision by United Auto Workers to opt for contractual security over a stake in technological changes in the Treaty of Detroit, although no doubt well-intended, proved myopic, and arguably jeopardised the future of thousands of auto workers. See Nick Dyer-Witheford, *Cyber-Proletariat: Global Labour in the Digital Vortex* (London: Pluto, 2015), pp. 39–41.

20. Naaman Zhou, 'It's a Tough Gig: Uber Drivers and Deliveroo Riders Fight for Employees' Rights', *Guardian*, 8 July 2017. See also Facility Waters and Jamie Woodcock,

'Far from Seamless: A Workers' Inquiry at Deliveroo', *Viewpoint Magazine*, 20 September 2017, at viewpoint mag.com.

21. Adam Barr, 'Microresistance: Inside the Day of a Supermarket Picker', *Notes from Below*, 20 March 2018, at notesfrombelow.org.

22. Aaron Benanav, *Automation and the Future of Work* (London/New York: Verso, 2020), p. 71.

23. Kolinko, 'Hotlines – Call Centre, Inquiry, Communism', *Libcom*, 2002, at libcom.org.

24. Ibid.

3 Management

1. Jonathan E. Cohn, 'Ultrasonic Bracelet and Receiver for Detecting Position in 2D Plane', 2017, US 2017/0278051 A1; Tye M. Brady, 'Wrist Band Haptic Feedback System', 2018, US 2017/0278052 A1.

2. SupplyChainDigest, 'Amazon Files Patent for Augmented Reality Putaway, Critics Again Erroneously Worry about Big Brother', 6 August 2018, at scdigest.com.

3. Mark Ellis, 'Amazon Under Fire for Patenting "Augmented Reality" Goggles to Spy on Workers and Make Them Work Harder', *Daily Mirror*, 3 August 2018.

4. Rebecca Hills-Duty, 'Amazon Files Patents Applications for Employee AR Goggles [Updated]', *VR Focus*, August 2018, at vrfocus.com.

5. For a biography, see Daniel A. Wren and Ronald G. Greenwood, *Management Innovators: The People and Ideas That Have Shaped Modern Business* (New York: Oxford University Press, 1998), pp. 134–40.

6. See also Ralph M. Barnes, *Motion and Time Study: Design and Measurement at Work* (New York: John Wiley, 1980), p. 14; Phoebe V. Moore, *The Quantified Self in Precarity:*

Work, Technology and What Counts (London/New York: Routledge, 2018), p. 47.

7. Milton J. Nadworny, *Scientific Management and the Unions, 1900–1932: A Historical Analysis* (Cambridge, MA: Harvard University Press, 1955), p. 49.

8. Harry Braverman, *Labor and Monopoly Capitalism: The Degradation of Work in the Twentieth Century* (New York/ London: Monthly Review, 1974), p. 54.

9. Frederick Winslow Taylor, *The Principles of Scientific Management* (New York/London: Harper, 1911).

10. Cooperation here refers to compliance more than collaboration. 'Cooperation' became a favoured slogan of employers during the industrial conflict of the period after the First World War, as noted in Reinhard Bendix, *Work and Authority in Industry: Ideologies of Management in the Course of Industrialization* (New York/Evanston: Harper & Row, 1963), p. 281. See also Gerard Hanlon, *The Dark Side of Management: A Secret History of Management Theory* (London/New York: Routledge, 2016), p. 26.

11. Taylor, *Principles of Scientific Management*, p. 17.

12. Many managers can fairly be considered 'workers of the means of production' in the vulgar sense, but that description alone would belie their relation to other workers.

13. Lillian Moller Gilbreth, *The Quest of the One Best Way: A Sketch of the Life of Frank Bunker Gilbreth* (Chicago: Society of Industrial Engineers, 1926), p. 34. See also Brian Price, 'Frank and Lillian Gilbreth and the Motion Study Controversy, 1907–1930', in Daniel Nelson, ed., *A Mental Revolution: Scientific Management Since Taylor* (Columbus, OH: Ohio State University Press, 1992), pp. 58–76.

14. Gilbreth, *Quest of the One Best Way*, p. 28.

15. Ibid., p. 25.

16. Price, 'Frank and Lillian Gilbreth', pp. 60–1.

17. Wren and Greenwood, *Management Innovators*, p. 143.
18. Taylor, *Principles of Scientific Management*, p. 62.
19. For more on the business competition between Taylor and the Gilbreths, see Price, 'Frank and Lillian Gilbreth', pp. 63–4.
20. Wren and Greenwood, *Management Innovators*, p. 171.
21. Ibid., pp. 172–5.
22. Lyndall F. Urwick, *The Life and Work of Elton Mayo* (London: Urwick, Orr & Partners, 1960), pp. 14–15.
23. Hanlon, *Dark Side of Management*, p. 143.
24. Taylor, *Principles of Scientific Management*, p. 5.
25. Ibid., p. 13.
26. Ibid., p. 15.
27. A function later to be carried out by what we now know as human resources management.
28. Hanlon, *Dark Side of Management*, pp. 95–6.
29. Price, 'Frank and Lillian Gilbreth', pp. 59–62.
30. Nadworny, *Scientific Management and the Unions*, pp. 22–3.
31. Ibid., p. 163.
32. Elton Mayo, *The Social Problems of Industrial Civilization* (London: Routledge & Kegan Paul, 1975), pp. 23–4.
33. Wren and Greenwood, *Management Innovators*, p. 175.
34. Mayo, *Social Problems of Industrial Civilization*, p. 61.
35. Hanlon, *Dark Side of Management*, p. 153.
36. Raniero Panzieri, 'Surplus Value and Planning: Notes on the Reading of Capital', 1976, at wordpress.com.
37. Hanlon, *Dark Side of Management*, pp. 3–14.
38. Ibid., p. 25.
39. Nick Dyer-Witheford, *Cyber-Proletariat: Global Labour in the Digital Vortex* (London: Pluto, 2015), pp. 51–3.
40. Michel de Certeau, *The Practice of Everyday Life* (Berkeley/Los Angeles: University of California Press, 1984), pp. 34–7. A strategy, for de Certeau, 'postulates a *place* that

can be delimited as its *own* and serve as a base from which relations with an *exteriority* composed of targets of threats ... can be managed'. He continues: 'As in management, every "strategic" rationalization seeks first of all to distingush its "own" place, that is, the place of its own power and will, from an "environment".' This is different from a tactic, which is 'a calculated action determined by the absence of a proper locus ... The space of a tactic is the space of the other'. He argues that the tactic is 'an art of the weak'.

41. See also Carter L. Goodrich, *The Frontier of Control: A Study in British Workshop Politics* (London: Pluto, 1975), p. 56.

42. The verb *to manage* comes from the Latin for hand, *manus*, via the French *manège*, in antiquated usage a riding hall for training horses. See Braverman, *Labor and Monopoly Capitalism*, p. 67.

43. Wren and Greenwood, *Management Innovators*, p. 151.

44. Dyer-Witheford, *Cyber-Proletariat*, p. 50.

45. Amazon, 'Kaizen', n.d., at aboutamazon.co.uk.

46. Kaoru Ishikawa, *What Is Total Quality Control? The Japanese Way* (Englewood Cliffs: Prentice-Hall, 1985), p. 151.

47. Ibid., p. 64.

48. Ibid., p. 5.

49. Hanlon, *Dark Side of Management*, p. 153.

50. *Panorama*, 'Amazon: The Truth Behind the Click', BBC, 25 November 2013.

51. Ibid.

52. Antonio Negri, *The Politics of Subversion: A Manifesto for the Twenty-First Century* (Cambridge: Polity, 1989), p. 106.

53. Andrew Pickering, *The Cybernetic Brain: Sketches of Another Future* (Chicago: Chicago University Press, 2010), p. 253.

54. Dyer-Witheford, *Cyber-Proletariat*, p. 42.

55. In contrast to the increasingly fashionable, though definitionally incorrect, use of 'performative' (where it is taken to mean 'insincere' or 'superficial'), Pickering has in mind the linguistic meaning of the term – namely, acts of communication that consummate action. See Pickering, *Cybernetic Brain*, p. 23.

56. Ibid., p. 383.

57. Ibid., pp. 20–3.

58. Ibid., pp. 222-3.

59. Ibid., p. 23.

60. Stafford Beer, *Brain of the Firm* (Chichester: John Wiley, 1981), p. 17.

61. Stafford Beer, *Cybernetics and Management* (London: English Universities Press, 1959), p. 17.

62. Pickering, *Cybernetic Brain*, p. 253.

63. Ibid., pp. 244, 253, 273.

64. Dyer-Witheford, *Cyber-Proletariat*, p. 42.

65. See Eden Medina, *Cybernetic Revolutionaries: Technology and Politics in Allende's Chile* (Cambridge, MA: MIT Press, 2014).

66. Pickering, *Cybernetic Brain*, p. 267.

67. Robert S. Kaplan and David P. Norton, *The Balanced Scorecard: Translating Strategy into Action* (Boston: Harvard Business School Press, 1996); Robert S. Kaplan, *Conceptual Foundations of the Balanced Scorecard (Working Paper)* (Boston: Harvard Business School, 2010), p. 28.

68. Pickering, *Cybernetic Brain*, p. 274.

69. Ibid., p. 273.

70. Pickering clarifies: 'a "purposive" system is a means to some extrinsically specified end, while a "purposeful" one can deliberate its own ends.' Ibid., p. 268. For Ulrich's critique, see Werner Ulrich, 'A Critique of Pure Cybernetic Reason: The Chilean Experience with Cybernetics', *Journal of Applied Systems Analysis* 8 (1981), p. 35.

71. To his credit, Beer did attempt to address this question in his later work on 'syntegration'.

72. Moore's conceptual use of 'agile' here transcends that of the 'Agile manifesto'. See Agile Alliance, 'Manifesto for Agile Software Development, 2001', at agilemanifesto.org. Situating contemporary management practices against older managerial forms such as scientific management and continuous improvement, Moore posits agile management as 'a form of total quality management and a high-performance work system'. The condition of 'agile workers' produced by this managerial form is reminiscent of Mark Fisher's description of contemporary work in *Capitalist Realism*: 'As production and distribution are restructured, so are nervous systems. To function effectively as a component of just-in-time production you must develop a capacity to respond to unforeseen events, you must learn to live in conditions of total instability'. See Mark Fisher, *Capitalist Realism: Is There No Alternative?* (Winchester: Zero Books, 2009), p. 34.

73. Moore, *Quantified Self*, p. 59.

74. Moore refers to an experimental project in which a single employee was able to produce over thirty gigabytes of data per week via three tracking devices.

75. Pickering, *Cybernetic Brain*, p. 23.

76. Klipfolio, 2015 'Guide to Business Dashboards', at klipfolio.com.

77. Ishikawa, *What Is Total Quality Control?*, p. 64.

78. Ned Rossiter, *Software, Infrastructure, Labor: A Media Theory of Logistical Nightmares* (New York/London: Routledge, 2016), p. 6.

79. Branden Hookway, *Interface* (Cambridge, MA/London: MIT Press, 2014).

80. The labour scholar Richard Edwards defines technical control as involving 'designing machinery and planning the flow of work to minimize the problem of transforming

labor power into labor as well as to maximize the purely physically based possibilities for achieving efficiencies.' See Richard Edwards, *Contested Terrain: The Transformation of the Workplace in the Twentieth Century* (New York: Basic Books, 1979), p. 112.

81. Florian Cramer and Matthew Fuller, 'Interface' in Matthew Fuller, ed., *Software Studies: A Lexicon* (Cambridge MA/ London: MIT Press, 2008), pp. 149–53.

82. Sally A. Applin and Michael D. Fischer, 'Watching Me, Watching You (Process Surveillance and Agency in the Workplace)', 2013, at posr.org.

83. Scott Lash, 'Power after Hegemony: Cultural Studies in Mutation?', in *Theory, Culture & Society* 23: 4 (2007), p. 71.

84. Melissa Gregg, *Work's Intimacy* (Cambridge: Polity, 2011). See also Natasha Dow Schüll, *Addiction by Design: Machine Gambling in Las Vegas* (Princeton/Oxford: Princeton University Press, 2012). Berardi clarifies: 'The soul I intend to discuss does not have much to do with the spirit. It is rather the vital breath that converts biological matter into an animated body. I want to discuss the soul in a materialistic way. What the body can do, that is its soul, as Spinoza said.' See Franco 'Bifo' Berardi, *The Soul at Work: From Alienation to Autonomy* (Los Angeles: Semiotext(e), 2009), p. 21.

85. Jamie Woodcock, 'Deliveroo and Precarious Work: The Labour Process and the Algorithmic Panopticon', at Digital Everyday Conference, King's College London, 6 May 2017. See also Jamie Woodcock, 'Automate This! Delivering Resistance in the Gig Economy', *Mute*, 10 March 2017, at metamute.org.

86. Harry Cleaver, *Reading Capital Politically* (Austin: University of Texas Press, 1979), pp. 42–3.

87. de Certeau, *Practice of Everyday Life*, p. 40.

4 Technological Politics

1. Karl Marx, *Capital: A Critique of Political Economy, Volume 1* (London: Penguin, 1990), pp. 554–5.

2. Harvey notes that this raises the question of what the 'technologies appropriate to a socialist or communist mode of production' are. See David Harvey, *A Companion to Marx's Capital* (London/New York: Verso, 2010), p. 218.

3. Ibid., p. 196. Here Harvey is attempting to move a dialectical-materialist framework beyond a narrow Hegelian dialectic between contradicting forces. Whether or not it is possible for such an amended framework still to be considered 'dialectical' is contestable. Personally, I am not invested in the structuralism implied by 'dialectical' Marxisms.

4. Ibid., pp. 195–6.

5. Harry Braverman, *Labor and Monopoly Capitalism: The Degradation of Work in the Twentieth Century* (New York/London: Monthly Review, 1974), p. 21.

6. Ibid., pp. 227–8.

7. Marx, *Capital, Volume 1*, p. 562.

8. Harry Cleaver, *Reading Capital Politically* (Austin: University of Texas Press, 1979), p. 15.

9. This is how Marx frames the period of technological recomposition following the working-class struggle for the shortening of the working day: '[It] gives an immense impetus to the development of productivity and the more economical use of the conditions of production. It imposes on the worker an increased expenditure of labour within a time which remains constant, a heightened tension of labour-power, and a closer filling-up of the pores of the working day, i.e. a condensation of labour, to a degree which can only be attained within the limits of the shortened working day.' In other words, the struggle forces capital to shift its focus from absolute surplus (the length

of labour time) to relative surplus (the 'condensation' of labour within a given time, that is, productivity), which it does through technological development to the detriment of workers' conditions: 'As soon as that shortening [of the working day] becomes compulsory, machinery becomes in the hands of capital the objective means, systematically employed, for squeezing out more labour in a given time.' See Marx, *Capital, Volume 1*, pp. 534–6. This is something we also see in the surge in manufacturing innovations in West Germany in the 1970s; the eventual result of 'trade-union power ... on sustained high wage rates, which produced a strong incentive for technological innovation'. See Harvey, *Companion to Marx's Capital*, pp. 213–14.

10. Cleaver, *Reading Capital Politically*, p. 28.
11. Langdon Winner, 'Do Artifacts Have Politics?', *Daedalus* 109: 1 (1980), pp. 121–36.
12. *Operaismo* is often inaccurately translated into English as 'workerism'. In contrast with *lavatore* (literally 'worker'), the alternative term *operaio* carries political connotations which are not captured by *lavatore*. 'Working class', for example, is *la classe operaia. Operaismo* presupposes class struggle, in that it suggests alignment with a political entity rather than the blinkered preoccupation with a particular sociological stratum implied by 'workerism'. *Operaismo* is also the collective term for the political movements from which the *operaisti* mentioned in this book emerged.
13. Cleaver, *Reading Capital Politically*, p. 53.
14. For an account of Panzieri in the English language, see Steve Wright, *Storming Heaven: Class Composition and Struggle in Italian Autonomist Marxism* (London: Pluto, 2002).
15. Karl Marx and Friedrich Engels, *The Communist Manifesto* (Harmondsworth: Penguin, 1967), p. 105.
16. Cleaver, *Reading Capital Politically*, p. 26.

17. Mario Tronti, 'Lenin in England', 1964, at marxists.org.

18. Harry Cleaver, 'Translators' Introductions: Part I', in Antonio Negri, *Marx Beyond Marx: Lessons from the Grundrisse* (New York: Autonomedia, 1991), p. xxiii.

19. Cleaver, *Reading Capital Politically*, pp. 42–3.

20. Marx, *Capital, Volume 1*, p. 508.

21. In the English language the most attentive history of this movement is Wright, *Storming Heaven*.

22. It should be noted here that *operaismo* (growing out of the *Quaderni Rossi* and *Classe Operaia* publications, and centred around the political group Potero Operaia) and, later on, *autonomia* (the subsequent flourishing – especially in the 1970s – of groups such as Autonomia Operaia, Lotta Continua, Lotta Femminista and the Radio Alice pirate station) were distinct movements with notable internal bifurcations. See, for example, Sergio Bologna, 'Review of Storming Heaven', 2005, at libcom.org.

23. Cleaver, *Reading Capital Politically*, pp. 4, 56, 10.

24. Wright, *Storming Heaven*, p. 41.

25. See Raniero Panzieri, 'Surplus Value and Planning: Notes on the Reading of Capital', 1976, at wordpress.com.

26. Marx, *Capital, Volume 1*, p. 563.

27. Winner, 'Do Artifacts Have Politics?', p. 124.

28. Nick Dyer-Witheford, *Cyber-Marx: Cycles and Circuits of Struggle in High-Technology Capitalism* (Urbana/Chicago, IL: University of Illinois Press, 1999), 71.

29. Winner, 'Do Artifacts Have Politics?', p. 127.

30. Dyer-Witheford, *Cyber-Marx*, pp. 70–1.

31. Winner, 'Do Artifacts Have Politics?', pp. 125–6.

32. Cleaver, *Reading Capital Politically*, 63.

33. Ibid., p. 25.

34. The example above is historically specific, and it should not be inferred that a self-activated political recomposition will automatically follow any shift in the technical composition

of the working class. But the point is that when the composition of the class changes, it does not mean that the potential for the class to act has been taken away, even if the specific means to act are no longer present, adequate or appropriate.

35. See Edward Andrew, 'Class in Itself and Class Against Capital: Karl Marx and His Signifiers', *Canadian Journal of Political Science/Revue canadienne de science politique* 16: 3 (1983), pp. 577–84.

36. Alberto Battaggia, 'Mass Worker and Social Worker: Reflections on the "New Class Composition"', 1981, at notesfrombelow.org.

37. Cleaver, *Reading Capital Politically*, p. 46.

38. This process and its political tensions are the subject of Elio Petri's 1965 film *La classe operaia va in paradiso* ('The Working Class Goes to Heaven').

39. See Paolo Virno, *A Grammar of the Multitude* (Los Angeles: Semiotext(e), 2004), pp. 110–11. Virno explores the idea that the epochal shift he marks out (not unproblematically) as the transition to 'post-Fordism' is capital's answer to the 'defeated revolution' of the 1970s, whereby capital delivered – in a deformed way – many of the demands typical of communism.

40. See Wright, *Storming Heaven*, pp. 46–7. Similarly, Lotta Femminista observed the effect of changes to the formal work process upon sections of the working class beyond 'the factory', particularly working-class women. In *Cyber-Marx*, Dyer-Witheford makes the useful point that workplace-orientated treatments of technology in general tend to ignore the effect of technological development on the wider class. These notions are most recently being reintroduced into class composition analyses by the British project Notes from Below, which is attempting to add a third vector of 'social composition' to contemporary perspectives.

41. Marx, *Capital, Volume 1*, p. 545.

42. Throughout this book I use the attributive 'workers inquiry' rather than the possessive 'workers' inquiry', although both are widely used. The discussion is staged at length by Christopher Wellbrook in 'A Workers' Inquiry or an Inquiry of Workers?', *Ephemera* 14: 3 (2014), pp. 73–99.

43. Raniero Panzieri, 'The Capitalist Use of Machinery: Marx Versus the Objectivists', 1980, pp. 5–7, at wordpress.com. These internal conflicts were to come to a head in Italy's 'hot autumn' of 1969, which 'brought out the growing separation between the struggles [of industrial and immigrant workers, students and women] and the Communist party/trade union hierarchies'. See Cleaver, *Reading Capital Politically*, p. 18. Similar divisions were apparent in the sewing machinists' struggle at Ford in Dagenham, and the struggles in Paris in May 1968.

44. Panzieri, 'Capitalist Use of Machinery', p. 10; Cleaver, *Reading Capital Politically*, p. 63.

45. See Fabrizio Fasulo, 'Raniero Panzieri and Workers' Inquiry: The Perspective of Living Labour, the Function of Science and the Relationship Between Class and Capital', *Ephemera* 14: 3 (2014), p. 318. See also Sandro Mancini, *Socialismo e democrazia diretta: Introduzione a Raniero Panzieri* (Bari: Dedalo Libri, 1977), p. 107.

46. Panzieri, 'Capitalist Use of Machinery', p. 3. This is despite the productive knowledge embodied by the machine having first been expropriated from the working class, as discussed in Chapter 3.

47. Maurizio Lazzarato, 'Immaterial Labor', in Paolo Virno and Michael Hardt, eds, *Radical Thought in Italy: A Potential Politics* (Minneapolis: University of Minnesota Press, 1996), pp. 134, 138–9.

48. Antonio Negri, *The Politics of Subversion: A Manifesto for the Twenty-First Century* (Cambridge: Polity, 1989), p. 77.

See also Antonio Negri, 'Archaeology and Project: The Mass Worker and Social Worker' (1971), in Antonio Negri, *Revolution Retrieved: Writings on Marx, Keynes, Capitalist Crisis and New Social Subjects (1967–83)* (London: Red Notes, 1988), p. 137.

49. Negri, *Politics of Subversion*, p. 78.

50. Battaggia, 'Mass Worker and Social Worker'.

51. Rodrigo Nunes, 'Forward How? Forward Where? (Post-) Operaismo Beyond the Immaterial Labour Thesis', *Ephemera* 7: 1 (2007), p. 200.

52. Dyer-Witheford, *Cyber-Proletariat*, pp. 10–11. See also Michael Hardt and Antonio Negri, *Empire* (Cambridge, MA: Harvard University Press, 2001).

53. As Aaron Bastani argues, digitally mediated 'connective action' is in any case no organisational panacea for political movements. See Aaron Peters, 'Strike! Occupy! Retweet! The Relationship Between Collective and Connective Action in Austerity Britain', DPhil thesis, Royal Holloway, University of London, 2015. See also Lance W. Bennett and Alexandra Segerberg, *The Logic of Connective Action: Digital Media and the Personalization of Contentious Politics* (Cambridge: Cambridge University Press, 2013).

54. Antonio Negri, 'Crisis of the Planner-State: Communism and Revolutionary Organisation' (1982), in Negri, *Revolution Retrieved*, p. 209. Emphasis in original.

55. Ibid.

56. Antonio Negri, 'Post-Operaismo? No, Operaismo', at University of Cambridge, 25 April 2017, and 'Who Are the Communists?' at SOAS, University of London, 26 April 2017.

57. Nunes, 'Beyond the Immaterial Labour Thesis', pp. 186–7.

58. Ibid., p. 190.

59. Sergio Bologna, '"Proletari e Stato" di Antonio Negri: una recensione', *Primo Maggio* 7 (1976), pp. 27–8; Wright, *Storming Heaven*, pp. 170–1.

60. Rivolta di classe, 'Letter aperta alla redazione milanese di "Rosso"' (1976), in Lucio Castellano, ed., *Aut. Op. La storia e i documenti: da Potere operaio all'Autonomia organizzata* (Rome: Savelli, 1980), p. 136; Wright, *Storming Heaven*, p. 171.

61. Ed Emery, 'No Politics Without Inquiry! A Proposal for a Class Composition Inquiry Project 1996–7', *Common Sense* 18 (1995), p. 2.

5 Algorithmic Management

1. Brody Ford, 'Uber Hires Prominent Critic to Focus on Treatment of Drivers', *Bloomberg*, 17 February 2021, at bloomberg.com.

2. Alex Rosenblat, *Uberland: How Algorithms Are Rewriting the Rules of Work* (Berkeley: University of California Press, 2018), p. 17.

3. Min Kyung Lee, Daniel Kusbit, Evan Metsky and Laura Dabbish, 'Working with Machines: The Impact of Algorithmic, Data-Driven Management on Human Workers', *Proceedings of the ACM/SIGCHI Conference on Human Factors in Computing Systems* (2015), pp. 1603–12, at dl.acm.org.

4. Ibid.

5. Lee's framing of the problem of transparency assumes the human-centredness we should be pursuing does not involve humans (that is, workers) centring themselves in their own decisions – 'maximizing individual benefit' – but instead privileging 'group optimization'. See Min Kyung Lee, 'Algorithmic Bosses, Robotic Colleagues: Toward Human-Centred Algorithmic Workplaces', *XRDS* 23: 2 (2016), pp. 42–7. It is unclear whether 'group optimization' means the most optimal set of arrangements for the 'system', the drivers collectively, or the company. But we can hazard a guess.

6. Tiziana Terranova, 'Red Stack Attack! Algorithms, Capital and the Automation of the Common', in Robin Mackay and Armen Avanessian, eds, *#Accelerate: The Accelerationist Reader* (Falmouth: Urbanomic, 2014), p. 384.

7. This leads Scholz to his position that the actual alternative to the 'individualist ethos of the "sharing economy"' is for workers to control platforms themselves, without managers. Scholz calls this idea 'platform cooperativism', as an alternative to the idea of 'platform capitalism'. See Trebor Scholz, *Uberworked and Underpaid: How Workers Are Disrupting the Digital Economy* (Cambridge: Polity, 2017), pp. 2–3. See also Nick Srnicek, *Platform Capitalism* (Cambridge: Polity, 2016).

8. Nick Seaver, 'What Should an Anthropology of Algorithms Do?', *Cultural Anthropology* 33: 3 (2018), p. 378.

9. This is despite its being advertised in terms of demand for drivers. See also Facility Waters and Jamie Woodcock, 'Far from Seamless: A Workers' Inquiry at Deliveroo', *Viewpoint Magazine*, 20 September 2017, at viewpointmag.com.

10. An added benefit to the employer is the reduced need for consistency (that is, retention) of personnel. Workplaces can have a fairly high turnover, attracting workers from student (Todd) and migrant (Lorenzo) labour pools from the local area, with seasonal contracts (José) or through agencies (Lorenzo). Where workplaces are located on industrial parks, such as in Greater London, it is not uncommon for workers to move between various distribution jobs all within close proximity to each other, which is possible in large part due to comparable ergonomic expectations.

11. The exception being the food-delivery platform, where logging in to the app *is* entering the workplace.

12. The food-delivery platform workflow, although vehicular, more closely resembles a warehouse-type workflow. As I

noted in Chapter 2, although the practicalities of platform work and warehouses are different, their form is similar; the app turns the town into a virtual warehouse for food-delivery riders.

13. There are occasions on which the consistency of work rhythms is interrupted by what appear to be technical irregularities – in such cases, workers are generally encouraged to contact a supervisor if one is available.

14. Franco 'Bifo' Berardi, *The Soul at Work: From Alienation to Autonomy* (Los Angeles: Semiotext(e), 2009), pp. 75–6.

15. See Jamie Barlett and Nathaniel Tkacz, *Governance by Dashboard: A Policy Paper* (London: Demos, 2017), p. 9n12.

16. We could speculate that a purely algorithmic system would see workers come on shift or be paid only when strictly necessary – an idea floating in the background of the cases that use flexible contracts or operate on a piece-rate model.

17. Plan C, 'Creatures of the Night: Changes in the Labour Process at Sainsbury's', 16 February 2017, at weareplanc. org.

18. Natasha Dow Schüll, *Addiction By Design: Machine Gambling in Las Vegas* (Princeton/Oxford: Princeton University Press, 2012), p. 49.

19. Ibid., p. 179.

20. Ned Rossiter, *Organized Networks: Media Theory, Creative Labour, New Institutions* (Rotterdam: NAi, 2006), p. 159.

21. *Panorama*, 'Amazon: The Truth Behind the Click', BBC, 25 November 2013.

22. The premise of the sci-fi thriller *Source Code* (dir. Duncan Jones, 2011) comes to mind, wherein the protagonist has a set amount of time to work out a puzzle before his timeline is reset to the beginning.

23. Ned Rossiter, *Software, Infrastructure, Labor: A Media Theory of Logistical Nightmares* (New York/London: Routledge, 2016), p. 40.
24. See Florian Cramer and Matthew Fuller, 'Interface', in Matthew Fuller, ed., *Software Studies: A Lexicon* (Cambridge, MA/London: MIT Press, 2008), p. 150.
25. See Carter L. Goodrich, *The Frontier of Control: A Study in British Workshop Politics* (London: Pluto, 1975), p. 56.
26. Matteo Pasquinelli, 'Anomaly Detection: The Mathematization of the Abnormal in Metadata Society', 2015, at academia.edu.
27. Maurizio Lazzarato, 'Immaterial Labor', in Paolo Virno and Michael Hardt, eds, *Radical Thought in Italy: A Potential Politics* (Minneapolis: University of Minnesota Press, 1996), p. 135.
28. Ibid.
29. Jesse LeCavalier, *The Rule of Logistics: Walmart and the Architecture of Fulfillment* (Minneapolis: University of Minnesota Press, 2016), pp. 40–3.
30. See Philip E. Agre, 'Surveillance and Capture: Two Models of Privacy', *Information Society* 10 (1994), p. 104.
31. See Branden Hookway, *Interface* (Cambridge, MA/London: MIT Press, 2014).
32. Goodrich, *Frontier of Control*, p. 56.
33. Shoshana Zuboff, 'Automate/Informate: The Two Faces of Intelligent Technology', *Organizational Dynamics*, 1985, at layoftheland.net.
34. She continues: 'The worker's knowledge had been implicit in his or her actions. Informating makes that knowledge explicit; it is a mirror reflecting what was tacitly known but now is in a form that is public and precise.' Zuboff's reading of Taylorism seems to take very literally scientific management's attitude to the conversion of worker's knowledge into managerial functions. However, Taylor

233

only listed the harvesting of knowledge as an example of managers' new responsibilities as part of a systematic approach to obtaining workers' 'initiative . . . with absolute uniformity'. See Frederick Winslow Taylor, *The Principles of Scientific Management* (New York/London: Harper, 1911), p. 15. Arguably, an informating technology would have been an ideal complement to Taylor's proposal.

35. See Shoshana Zuboff, *In the Age of the Smart Machine: The Future of Work and Power* (New York: Basic, 1988). See also Shosana Zuboff, 'Big Other: Surveillance Capitalism and the Prospects of an Information Civilisation', *Journal of Information Technology* 30 (2015), p. 81.

36. Jamie Woodcock, 'Deliveroo and Precarious Work: The Labour Process and the Algorithmic Panopticon', at King's College, London, 6 May 2017.

37. Scott Lash, 'Power after Hegemony: Cultural Studies in Mutation?' in *Theory, Culture & Society* 23: 4 (2007), pp. 70–1.

38. See Alexander R. Galloway, 'Protocol', *Theory, Culture & Society* 23: 2–3 (2006), pp. 317–20.

39. For example: if the system tells Todd to pick Marmite and Todd sees there is no Marmite, he uses his handset to tell the system Marmite is out of stock. Either the handset will suggest he choose Vegemite or another yeast extract, or he may tell the system he has selected Vegemite as an appropriate replacement. To ensure no other workers have to go through this process, and possessing the new information that there is no Marmite (whatever the stock database may have said before), the system will change the shopping manifests of other pickers, telling them to pick Vegemite rather than have them look for Marmite at all. After Todd has performed an 'item replacement', his colleagues will be unaware they were ever initially supposed to be looking for Marmite in the first place.

40. For an early discussion of this dynamic, see Zuboff, *In the Age of the Smart Machine*, pp. 337–55.
41. The humanistic management tradition has not necessarily been associated with a humane management tradition. For a fuller discussion, see Gerard Hanlon, *The Dark Side of Management: A Secret History of Management Theory* (London/New York: Routledge, 2016).
42. David Beer, 'The Social Power of Algorithms', *Information, Communication & Society* 20: 1 (2016), p. 996.
43. Franco Piperno, 'Technological Innovation and Sentimental Education', in Paolo Virno and Michael Hardt, eds, *Radical Thought in Italy: A Potential Politics* (Minneapolis: University of Minnesota Press, 1996), p. 127.
44. It is useful here to recall Bendix's reading of Taylor, which argues that one of Taylor's objectives was in fact to eliminate personal managerial authority through a greater adherence to an authoritative 'science': 'Once his methods had been introduced, the managers would be as much subject to rules and discipline as the workers themselves . . . Thus cooperation resulted from the fact that workers and managers complied with the results of scientific investigations, though it also depended upon a prior mental revolution which made the wholehearted acceptance of these results possible.' See Reinhard Bendix, *Work and Authority in Industry: Ideologies of Management in the Course of Industrialization* (New York/Evanston: Harper & Row, 1963), p. 278.
45. Waters and Woodcock, 'Far from Seamless'.
46. See Cramer and Fuller, 'Interface', pp. 150–1.
47. For an in-depth discussion of SAP, the leading brand of enterprise resource software globally, see Rossiter, *Software, Infrastructure, Labor*, pp. 51–6.
48. Alex Rosenblat and Luke Stark, 'Algorithmic Labor and Information Asymmetries: A Case Study of Uber's Drivers',

International Journal of Communication 10: 27 (2016), pp. 3762–3.

49. Min Kyung Lee, 'Understanding Perception of Algorithmic Decisions: Fairness, Trust, and Emotion in Response to Algorithmic Management', *Big Data & Society* 5: 1 (2018), pp. 1–16.

50. Lilian Edwards and Michael Veale, 'Slave to the Algorithm? Why a "Right to an Explanation" Is Probably Not the Remedy You Are Looking For', *Duke Law & Technology Review* 16 (2017), pp. 18–84.

51. Antonio Negri, 'Who Are the Communists?' at SOAS, University of London, 26 April 2017. The metaphor is likely a reference to the dual meaning of *manège*, originally from French.

52. Mark Fisher, *Capitalist Realism: Is There No Alternative?* (Winchester: Zero, 2009), p. 34.

53. Waters and Woodcock, 'Far from Seamless'. See also Roger Clarke, 'Information Technology and Dataveillance', *Communications of the ACM* 31: 5 (1988), pp. 498–512; and Sara Degli Eposti, 'When Big Data Meets Dataveillance: The Hidden Side of Analytics', *Surveillance & Society* 12: 2 (2014), pp. 209–25.

54. Harry Cleaver, *Reading Capital Politically* (Austin: University of Texas Press, 1979), p. 43.

6 Guile against Adversity

1. Clare Hymer, 'Welcome to Slacker School: Learning from the Best How to Work the Least', *Novara Media*, 3 June 2021, at novaramedia.com. See also Rivkah Brown, 'Paranoid Bosses Are Spying on Workers During the Pandemic', *Novara Media*, 10 February 2021, at novaramedia.com.

2. Stephen Ackroyd and Paul Thompson, *Organizational Misbehaviour* (London: Sage, 1999), p. 23.

3. Harry Braverman, *Labor and Monopoly Capitalism: The Degradation of Work in the Twentieth Century* (New York/London: Monthly Review, 1974), p. 17.

4. David Collinson and Stephen Ackroyd, 'Resistance, Misbehaviour, and Dissent', in Stephen Ackroyd, Rosemary Batt, Paul Thompson and Pamela S. Tolbert, eds, *The Oxford Handbook of Work and Organization* (Oxford: Oxford University Press, 2005), p. 321.

5. Ackroyd and Thompson, *Organizational Misbehaviour*, p. 5.

6. Randy Hodson, 'Worker Resistance: An Underdeveloped Concept in the Sociology of Work', *Economic and Industrial Democracy* 16: 1 (1995), p. 80.

7. Collinson and Ackroyd, 'Resistance, Misbehaviour, and Dissent', p. 321. See also Dorinne K. Kondo, *Crafting Selves: Power, Gender and Discourses of Identity in a Japanese Workplace* (Chicago: University of Chicago Press, 1990), p. 224.

8. Jamie Woodcock, *Working the Phones: Control and Resistance in Call Centres* (London: Pluto, 2017), p. 109.

9. See James C. Scott, *Seeing Like a State: How Certain Schemes to Improve the Human Condition Have Failed* (New Haven, CT: Yale University Press, 2005), pp. 112–13.

10. Mario Tronti, 'The Strategy of Refusal' (1965), in Sylvère Lotringer and Christian Marazzi, eds, *Autonomia: Post-Political Politics* (Los Angeles: Semiotext(e), 2007).

11. Michael Hardt and Antonio Negri, *Empire* (Cambridge, MA: Harvard University Press, 2001), p. 204.

12. Mario Tronti, 'The Struggle against Labor', 1972, at la.utexas.edu.

13. Ibid.

14. Woodcock, *Working the Phones*, pp. 98–100.

15. James C. Scott, *Domination and the Arts of Resistance:*

Hidden Transcripts (New Haven/London: Yale University Press, 2005), p. 183.

16. For a more detailed account of this action, see Angry Workers, *Class Power on Zero-Hours* (London: Angry Workers, 2020).

17. Braverman, *Labor and Monopoly Capitalism*, p. 35.

18. Paul Thompson and Stephen Ackroyd, 'All Quiet on the Workplace Front? A Critique of Recent Trends in British Industrial Sociology', *Sociology* 29: 4 (1995), p. 629.

19. Due to the lack of direct translation, μῆτις is variously transliterated as *metis*, *mêtis* and *mētis* within anglophone literature.

20. Benedict Singleton, 'On Craft and Being Crafty', PhD thesis, Northumbria University, 2014, pp. 102–7.

21. Marcel Detienne and Jean-Pierre Vernant, *Cunning Intelligence in Greek Culture and Society* (Chicago: University of Chicago Press, 1991), pp. 3–4.

22. Woodcock, *Working the Phones*, p. 104.

23. Michel de Certeau, *The Practice of Everyday Life* (Berkeley/Los Angeles: University of California Press, 1984), pp. 26–39. See also Michel de Certeau, 'On the Oppositional Practices of Everyday Life', *Social Text* 3 (1980), pp. 36–8.

24. Frederick Winslow Taylor, *The Principles of Scientific Management* (New York/London: Harper, 1911), pp. 6–8.

25. Min Kyung Lee, Daniel Kusbit, Evan Metsky and Laura Dabbish, 'Working with Machines: The Impact of Algorithmic, Data-Driven Management on Human Workers', *Proceedings of the ACM/SIGCHI Conference on Human Factors in Computing Systems* (2015), pp. 1603–12, at dl.acm.org.

26. Woodcock, *Working the Phones*, p. 107.

27. Alessio Lunghi, 'Counter Logistics and the Transnational Social Strike', *Transnational Social Strike Platform*, 2017, p. 49.

28. Transnational Social Strike Platform, *Logistics and the*

Transnational Social Strike, 2017, p. 9. See also Keir Milburn, 'On Social Strikes and Directional Demands', *Plan C*, 7 May 2015, at weareplanc.org.

29. Singleton, 'On Craft and Being Crafty', pp. 108–9.
30. Transnational Social Strike Platform, *Logistics and the Transnational Social Strike*.
31. See Scott, *Domination and the Arts of Resistance*, p. xii.
32. Plan C, 'Saboteurs on the Tills', 2 April 2017, at weareplanc .org.
33. And yet Taylorism fails to subsume these commons, mostly because it assumes the possibility of managers obtaining 'with absolute uniformity' the '"initiative" of the workmen'. See Taylor, *Principles of Scientific Management*, pp. 8–15. Although Taylor identifies the realm of 'traditional knowledge', which is something of a mystery to managers (to their detriment), his solutions presuppose the content of that 'traditional knowledge' before they gather it. The possibility of the continuous expansion or constant change in the content of knowledge to be gathered is the insight of both human relations and total quality control/*kaizen* approaches. These are underdeveloped in distribution workplaces – and in any case fallible – and exist mostly as ideological set pieces. Nonetheless, the assumption of even the most sophisticated algorithmic management infrastructures is that these factors can more or less be either captured or mediated by computational devices. What we are left with is a management apple picker, but workers who are dealing in both apples and oranges.
34. Woodcock, *Working the Phones*, p. 106.
35. Drawing on game studies, James Allen-Robertson discusses the example of 'rule discovery' among Uber drivers, as they learn the limits of the algorithmic infrastructure through interaction. See James Allen-Robertson, 'The Uber Game:

Exploring Algorithmic Management and Resistance', at 18th Annual Conference of the Association of Internet Researchers, 18–21 October 2017.

7 Epilogue

1. Derek Robertson, 'What Workers Want from Tech', *Politico*, 12 January 2023, at politico.com.

Index

Ackroyd, Stephen 179,
198, 236n2, 237nn4–5,
7, 238n18
Agre, Philip E. 233n30
Alabama 20
Allende, Salvador 96, 97
Allen-Robertson, James
239n35
Alquati, Romano 119,
126, 128, 129
Althusser, Louis 118
Amazon 3, 4, 10, 18,
19–21, 43, 62, 63, 64,
70, 81, 84, 85–92,
143–7, 152, 159–61,
178, 185, 186, 220n45
American Strategic Organ-
izing Center 210
Andrew, Edward 227n35
Applin, Sally 105, 223n82
Asda 53
Asos 18, 50

Bad Hersfeld, Germany 20
Ballantyne, Amanda 211
Barlett, Jamie 232n15

Barnes, Ralph M. 217n6
Barr, Adam 13, 58, 214n5,
217n21
Bastani, Aaron 229n53
Battaggia, Alberto
227n36, 229n50
BBC *Panorama* 88, 152
Beer, David 170, 235n42
Beer, Stafford 94, 95–6,
97, 99, 221nn60–1,
222n71
Benanav, Aaron 60,
217n22
Bendix, Reinhard 218n10,
235n44
Bennett, Lance W. 229n53
Bentham, Jeremy 106
Berardi, Franco 'Bifo' 106,
149, 223n84, 232n14
Bloomberg 138
Boewe, Jorn 215n6
Bologna, Sergio 136,
226n22, 229n59
Brady, Tye M. 217n1
Braverman, Harry 52, 66,
112–13, 118, 179, 198,

Braverman, Harry (*cont.*)
216n16, 218n8,
220n42, 224n5, 237n3,
238n17
Britain 7, 18–22, 50, 51
Brown, Rivkah 236n1
Bundy, Michael E. 216n14
Business, Energy and
Industrial Strategy
committee 56
Butler, Sarah 215n9

Career Choice Program
(Amazon) 86
Castellano, Lucio 230n60
CitySprint 49, 56
Classe Operaia 129
Cleaver, Harry 108,
113–14, 116–18, 119,
120, 123, 124, 128,
175, 223n86, 224n8,
225nn10, 13, 16,
226nn18–19, 23, 32,
227n37, 228n43,
236n54
Coal Commission 11
Cohn, Jonathan E. 217n1
Collinson, David 237nn4, 7
Comitati Autonomi
Operai 1 36–7
Covid-19 pandemic 178
Cramer, Florian 104,
223n81, 233n24,
235n46

Csikszentmihalyi, Mihaly
152

Dabbish, Laura 215n5,
230n3, 238n25
Darrow, John E. 216n14
De Certeau, Michel 80,
108, 200, 219–20n40,
223n87, 238n23
Deliveroo 3, 21, 44, 45,
48, 57, 106, 107,
144–7, 172, 178
Detienne, Marcel 199,
238n21
Dunayevskaya, Raya 126
Dyer-Witheford, Nick
79–80, 81, 92, 123,
214n3, 216n19,
219n39, 220nn44, 54,
221n66, 226nn28, 30,
227n40, 229n52

Edwards, Lilian 174,
236n50
Edwards, Richard 222–
3n80
Elaine (worker) 25, 26,
53, 54
Ellis, Mark 217n3
Emery, Ed 137, 230n61
Engels, Friedrich 225n15
Eposti, Sara Degli 236n53

Facebook 52

Fasulo, Fabrizio 228n45
Fischer, Michael D. 105,
    223n82
Fisher, Mark 1, 10, 13,
    174–5, 214n6, 222n72,
    236n52
Flex (Amazon) 143–7
Foodora 21
Ford, Brody 230n1
Foucault, Michel 106
Friedman, Bill 151
Fuller, Matthew 104,
    223n81, 233n24,
    235n46

Gall, Gregor 215n6
Galloway, Alexander R.
    234n38
General Electric Company
    73–4
General Motors 12
Germany 20, 129
Gilbreth, Frank Bunker
    68–70, 80
Gilbreth, Lillian Moller
    68, 69, 73, 84, 218n13
Glick, David D. 216n14
GMB 49, 50, 51–3, 56,
    63, 178
Goodrich, Carter L. 11,
    62, 162, 214n1,
    220n41, 233nn25, 32
Google Maps 38
Gopuff 29, 35

Greenwood, Ronald G.
    217n5, 219nn17, 20,
    33, 220n43
Gregg, Melissa 223n84
GrubHub 3

Hanlon, Gerard 77, 79,
    218n10, 219nn22, 28,
    35, 219n37, 220n49,
    235n41
Hardt, Michael 133,
    229n52, 237n11
Harvey, David 110–12,
    224nn2–4, 225n9
Heathrow service area,
    London 29
Hills-Duty, Rebecca
    217n4
Hodson, Randy 179,
    237n6
Hookway, Branden 103,
    162, 183, 222n79,
    233n31
House of Lords 11
Hymer, Clare 236n1

Independent Workers'
    Union of Great Britain
    (IWGB) 46, 49, 50, 57,
    178
Invisible Committee 209
Ishikawa, Kaoru 82, 83,
    100, 220n46, 222n77
Italy 20, 21, 126, 128

James, C. L. R. 126
Jamie (worker) 45, 46, 48,
    101, 144, 172, 174,
    185, 196
Johnson-Forest Tendency
    126
José (worker) 70–3, 88,
    143, 144, 155, 159,
    169, 186

Kaizen programme
    (Amazon) 81
Kaplan, Robert S. 97, 99,
    221n67
Klipfolio 100, 222n76
Kolinko 60, 61, 217n23
Kondo, Dorinne K. 237n7
Kusbit, Daniel 215n5,
    230n3, 238n25

Lash, Scott 106, 164,
    223n83, 234n37
Lazzarato, Maurizio
    131, 158–9, 228n47,
    233n27
LeCavalier, Jesse 40, 160,
    216n13, 233n29
Lee, Min Kyung 174,
    215n5, 230nn3, 5,
    236n49, 238n25
Lenin, Vladimir 110
Lorenzo (worker) 29–32,
    36–9, 49, 100, 101,
    144, 154–7, 166, 173,

184, 186, 188–91, 195,
    196, 197, 198, 200
Lotta Femminista 128,
    227n40
LTN2 fulfilment centre
    (Amazon) 85–6
Lunghi, Alessio 238n27
Lyft 3, 139, 140, 142

Madan, Udit 216n14
#MakeAmazonPay
    campaign 22
Mancini, Sandro 228n45
Marx, Karl 64, 76, 109,
    110, 111, 113, 116,
    118, 121, 130, 224nn1,
    7, 224–5nn9, 15,
    226nn20, 26, 228n41
Mayo, Elton 74, 75,
    78–80, 82, 84,
    219nn32, 34
McCormick Harvesting
    Machine Company 122,
    124
Metsky, Evan 215n5,
    230n3, 238n25
Midvale Steel Works 65
Milburn, Keir 239n28
Montaldi, Danilo 119
Moody, Kim 18, 214n3
Moore, Phoebe 28, 99,
    216n12, 217n6,
    222nn72–4
Motorola MC3000 87

Motorola WT4000 device 30, 105

Nadworny, Milton J. 218n7, 219n30
Negri, Antonio 91, 119, 123, 131, 133–5, 136, 174, 220n52, 228–9n48, 229nn49, 52, 54–6, 236n51, 237n11
New York 20
Noah (worker) 45, 46, 47, 101, 144, 145, 166, 174, 185, 196
Northumberland Miners' Association 11
Norton, David P. 221n67
Nunes, Rodrigo 132, 135, 229n51, 57

Obama, Barack 86
O'Connor, Sarah 214n4
Office for National Statistics 216n17
Ohno, Taiichi 81
Osborne, Hilary 215n9

Panzieri, Raniero 27, 115–16, 119, 120–1, 123, 128–9, 130, 211, 219n36, 225n14, 226n25, 228nn43–4, 46
Pasquinelli, Matteo 156, 233n26

Peters, Aaron 229n53
Petri, Elio 227n38
Pickering, Andrew 91, 93–4, 97, 98, 220n53, 221nn55, 62, 68–70, 222n75
Pinochet, General 97
Piperno, Franco 171–2, 235n43
Plato 202–3
Poland 21
Price, Brian 218n13, 219nn19, 29
Price, Mark 14
Project CyberSyn 96–7
Pulse (Deliveroo) 144–7

Quaderni Rossi 126, 129

Reuther, Walter 12
Robertson, Derek 240n1
Romano, Paul 128
Rosenblat, Alex 138, 215n5, 230n2, 235n48
Rossiter, Ned 102, 152, 222n78, 232n20, 233n23, 235n47

Sainsbury 150
sat-nav 37, 38, 39
Scholz, Trebor 142, 231n7
Schüll, Natasha Dow 151–2, 223n84, 232n18
Schulten, Johannes 215n6

Scott, James C. 183,
237nn9, 15, 239n31
Seaver, Nick 143, 231n8
Segerberg, Alexandra
229n53
Silver, Laura 215n4
Singleton, Benedict 199,
202, 238n20, 239n29
Source Code (film)
232n22
South Yorkshire, England
2
Soviet Union 110
Spain 20, 21
Spary, Sara 215n4
Sports Direct 18
Starbucks 135–6
Stark, Luke 215n5,
235n48
Stone, Ria 14, 128
Straker, William 11
SupplyChainDigest web-
site 63, 217n2

Taylor, Frederick Winslow
65–9, 73, 75–81, 105,
201, 205, 218nn9, 11,
219nn18, 24, 233–
4n34, 235n44, 238n24,
239n33
Terranova, Tiziana 231n6
Thompson, Paul 179, 198,
236n2, 237n5, 238n18
Tkacz, Nathaniel 232n15

Todd (worker) 33–6, 54,
55, 101, 157, 161, 165,
167, 168, 169, 187–9,
192–5, 198, 200, 201,
202, 234n39
Trades Union Congress
(Britain) 210
Transnational Social
Strike Platform 238n28,
239n30
Tronti, Mario 117, 119,
121, 181–2, 226n17,
237nn10, 12
TUC 22, 50

Uber 3, 49, 50, 51, 56, 57,
138–9, 140, 142, 201
Uber Eats 21
Ueno, Yoichi 80–1
Ulrich, Werner 98, 221n70
Unite 63
United Auto Workers 12,
216n19
United States 7, 20, 21,
70, 110
United Voices of the
World 50
Urwick, Lyndall F. 75,
219n22
Usdaw 51, 54, 178

Veale, Michael 174,
236n50
Ver.di union 20

Vernant, Jean-Pierre 199, 238n21
Virno, Paolo 227n39

Waitrose 14
Walmart 15, 53
Waters, Facility 175, 216n20, 231n9, 235n45, 236n53
Wellbrook, Christopher 228n42
Western Electric Company 73
White House 210
Wiener, Norbert 12
Winner, Langdon 114–15, 122, 225n11, 226nn27, 29, 31
Woodcock, Jamie 106–7, 108, 164, 175, 181, 200, 206, 216n20, 223n85, 231n9,

234n36, 235n45, 236n53, 237nn8, 14, 238nn22, 26, 239n34
Wren, Daniel A. 217n5, 219nn17, 20, 33, 220n43
Wright, Steve 225n14, 226nn21, 24, 227n40, 230n60
Wrigley's Juicy Fruit chewing gum 40
Writers Guild of America West 209, 210, 211

XPO 50

Yorkshire, England 23

Zhou, Naaman 216n20
Zuboff, Shoshana 163, 175, 233nn33–4, 234n35, 235n40